Experience
Physics

Physics and Math
Skills Workbook

SAVVAS
LEARNING COMPANY

ISBN-13: 978-1-4183-3398-0
ISBN-10: 1-4183-3398-0

4   22

TABLE OF CONTENTS

Welcome to the Physics Math and Skills Workbook

The *Physics and Math Skills Workbook* consists of a review of each investigation in your Student Handbook, presented in order of the learning experiences. As part of this review, the Skills Workbook provides you with practice questions to help you develop science and math skills.

The **science skills** covered by the Skills Workbook include the following Science and Engineering Practices:

- Asking Questions and Defining Problems
- Developing and Using Models
- Analyzing and Interpreting Data
- Constructing Explanations and Designing Solutions
- Engaging in Argument from Evidence

The **math skills** covered by the Skills Workbook include the following:

- Make sense of problems and persevere in solving them
- Reason abstractly and quantitatively
- Construct viable arguments and critique the reasoning of others
- Model with mathematics
- Use appropriate tools strategically
- Attend to precision
- Look for and make use of structure
- Look for and express regularity in repeated reasoning

The questions and the problems in this Workbook also help you develop other skills and an overall understanding of the material.

Displacement and Velocity

In physics, the quantities known as displacement and velocity are essential to describing the motion of an object. Once an object's position is defined relative to a coordinate system, the following definitions are used:

Displacement	Velocity
$\Delta d = d_f - d_i$	$v = \dfrac{\Delta d}{\Delta t}$
Δd = displacement d_f = final position d_i = initial position	v = velocity Δd = displacement Δt = change in time

If you were to construct a graph with position on the vertical axis and time on the horizontal axis, you should recognize that the definition of velocity is equivalent to the slope of a position vs. time graph. The familiar term "speed" is used to refer to the magnitude or absolute value of the velocity.

The slope of each of these line segments corresponds to the velocity of the moving object.

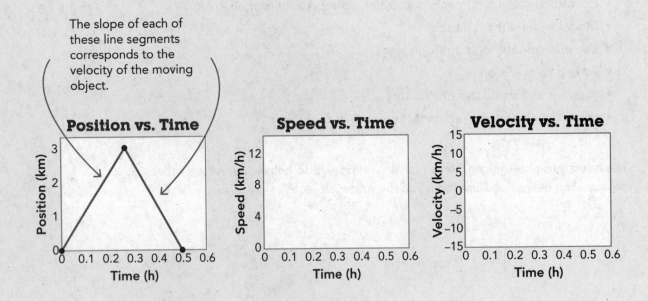

Analyzing and Interpreting Data The slope of each of the line segments in the position vs. time graph corresponds to the velocity of the moving object. Use the points on the position vs. time graph to calculate the slopes of the line segments and use this to complete the graphs of speed vs. time and velocity vs. time. Be careful figuring out the coordinates of the highest point on the position vs. time graph.

Mathematical Practices:
Reason Abstractly and Quantitatively

If an object moves in two dimensions rather than just along a straight line, the displacement can be represented either in terms of components relative to a set of x and y axes or by a vector with a magnitude (length) that is related to the x and y components by the Pythagorean theorem.

To write the displacement in terms of components, the symbols $\hat{x}$ and $\hat{y}$ (read aloud as x-hat and y-hat) are used to indicate, respectively, "in the x direction" and "in the y direction." These symbols represent vectors in their respective directions that have a magnitude of 1 and are referred to as *unit vectors*. So, to indicate a displacement of 24 m in the positive x direction and 12 m in the negative y direction, you would write

$$d = (24 \text{ m})\hat{x} + (-12 \text{ m})\hat{y}$$

This abstract representation of a two-dimensional displacement can be visualized and then treated mathematically by drawing a right triangle with the two components as the two perpendicular sides and the displacement as the hypotenuse.

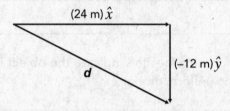

Since the x and y components are perpendicular, the length of the displacement vector, $|d|$, can be calculated using the familiar formula for a right triangle (the Pythagorean Theorem):

$$d^2 = a^2 + b^2$$

$$|d| = \sqrt{a^2 + b^2} = \sqrt{(24 \text{ m})^2 + (-12 \text{ m})^2} = 26.8 \text{ m}$$

Notice that the displacement is not simply the sum of the two components because they are in different directions.

3-Dimensional Review

1. DCI Forces and Motion Describe, in your own words, displacement, speed, and velocity.

_____

_____

_____

_____

2. SEP Analyzing and Interpreting Data Answer the following questions about the data based on an object in motion:

Time (s)	0	1	2	3
Position (m)	0	1	4	9

a. Draw a position graph of the data. Does this demonstrate uniform or non-uniform motion? Explain your answer.

_____

_____

b. Draw a dot diagram for the position graph. Does this indicate the object is speeding up, slowing down, or having uniform motion?

_____

_____

c. Based on your previous answers, is the velocity positive or negative? Explain your answer.

_____

_____

3. CCC Cause and Effect A small cart is sitting at its starting point in the middle of a straight track. If you give the cart a push in the positive direction, what will happen to the cart? Circle all that apply.

a. The speed of the cart will increase.

b. The displacement of the cart will decrease.

c. The velocity of the cart will increase.

d. The displacement of the cart will increase.

e. The velocity of the cart will decrease.

Skills Practice

4. Starting from one shore, you swim east across a narrow river to the other shore. The river is 19.0 m wide. As you swim, the river current moves you north up the river a distance of 12.0 m. Draw a diagram representing this situation. What is your resultant displacement? Express your answer in components, and then determine the magnitude.

5. A child releases a balloon at a park. The balloon travels up into the air 8.20 m, and east across the park a distance of 23.0 m, before getting stuck in a tree. Draw a diagram representing this situation. What is the resultant displacement of the balloon? Express your answer in components, and then determine the magnitude.

6. A bird drops a feather from the roof of a 13.1 m tall building. The feather is blown 48.6 m west before falling to the ground. What is the resultant displacement of the balloon?

a. 7.90 m

b. 10.6 m

c. 61.7 m

d. 50.3 m

Acceleration

If you watch any moving object long enough, you are likely to observe a change in the object's velocity due to a change in either the speed or the direction of motion. Since velocity is related to the slope of a position vs. time graph, an object with a changing velocity might have a curved position vs. time graph similar to the one shown below.

| The slope of a tangent to each point on this graph is the instantaneous velocity. | The slope of this graph is the acceleration. |

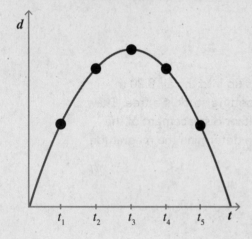

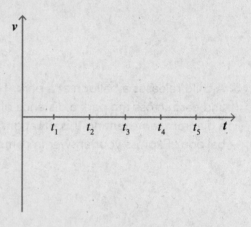

The term acceleration is used in physics to refer to the rate of change of velocity.

Acceleration

$$a = \frac{v_2 - v_1}{t_2 - t_1} = \frac{\Delta v}{\Delta t}$$

a = acceleration $\qquad \Delta t$ = change in time

Δv = change in velocity

Similar to the definition of velocity as the slope of a displacement vs. time graph, this equation can be interpreted to define acceleration as the rate of change of the velocity or the slope of a velocity vs. time graph.

Develop and Use Models Draw a tangent line at each of the indicated points on the position vs. time graph. Compare the slopes and use them to plot points that would produce a linear velocity vs. time graph. Use the velocity vs. time graph to explain whether the acceleration of this object is positive or negative.

Mathematical Practices: Persevere in Solving Problems

When working in physics, you may find that you don't have an equation that you can apply to directly solve a problem using only the given information. In such cases, you may need to use one equation to generate an intermediate answer and then use that answer in a second equation to solve the problem.

Suppose that a highway engineer wants to calculate the length of an on-ramp so that a car accelerating from rest at a rate of 3.6 m/s² is able to reach a velocity of 28 m/s forward at the end of the ramp.

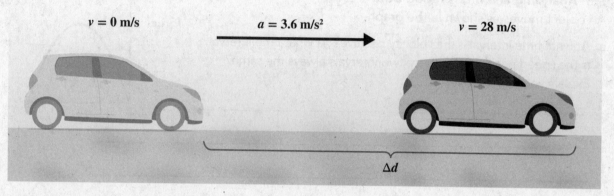

The engineer knows the following two equations of motion:

Equation of Motion (Velocity)		Equation of Motion (Displacement)	
$v = v_i + at$		$\Delta d = v_i t + \frac{1}{2}at^2$	
v = velocity	a = acceleration	Δd = displacement	t = time
v_i = initial velocity	t = time	v_i = initial velocity	a = acceleration

The engineer can't solve the displacement equation of motion because the time isn't part of the given information. However, it is possible to use the velocity equation of motion to solve for time, since the final velocity (28 m/s) and the acceleration (3.6 m/s²) are given, and the initial velocity can be inferred to be zero based on the words "from rest." Here's how the engineer would solve that equation for time:

$$v - v_i = at$$

$$t = \frac{v - v_i}{a} = \frac{28 \text{ m/s} - 0 \text{ m/s}}{3.6 \text{ m/s}^2} = 7.8 \text{ s}$$

Once the time is known, the engineer can substitute that value along with the initial velocity and the acceleration into the displacement equation to calculate the length of the on-ramp:

$$\Delta d = v_i t + \frac{1}{2}at^2 = (0 \text{ m/s})(7.8 \text{ s}) + \frac{1}{2}(3.6 \text{ m/s}^2)(7.8 \text{ s})^2 = 110 \text{ m}$$

If there isn't an obvious route to solving a problem, consider what you can determine from the given information and whether that could be used to help generate a final solution.

3-Dimensional Review

1. DCI Forces and Motion A ball is rolling down a flat, frictionless ramp with a constant velocity of 13 m/s. What is the acceleration of the ball over three seconds? Over an infinite number of seconds? Explain your answer.

_____

_____

_____

2. SEP Analyzing and Interpreting Data
An object moves as shown in the graph.

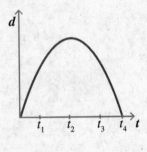

a. At what time interval is the velocity positive? At what time interval is the speed positive? Are these two intervals always the same? Explain your answer.

_____

_____

_____

_____

b. Based on the velocity, over what time interval is the acceleration constant? Draw a velocity graph to explain your answer.

_____

_____

_____

_____

c. Assume each time interval (t_1, t_2, t_3, t_4) is one second. If the velocity at t_1 is 13 m/s, what is the acceleration?

_____

_____

3. CCC Cause and Effect A cart rolling down a metal track at a constant rate of 8.2 m/s encounters a patch of sand causing an acceleration of −0.6 m/s². After 2 seconds, which of the following is correct? Circle all that apply.

a. Displacement of the cart will be −1.2 m   **b.** Displacement of the cart be 15.2 m

c. Velocity of the cart will be 7.0 m/s   **d.** Velocity of the cart will be 7.6 m/s

Skills Practice

4. A highway engineer wants to calculate the length of an on-ramp so that a car accelerating from rest at a rate of 12.4 m/s² is able to reach a velocity of 20.0 m/s at the end of the ramp. How long must the on-ramp be to meet these conditions?

5. An engineer wants to calculate how high a rocket starting from rest will be when it reaches a velocity of 6,500.0 m/s with an acceleration of 389.00 m/s². How high will the rocket be when it meets these conditions?

6. A student wants to calculate how far his boxcar starting from rest will go when it reaches an acceleration of 13.1 m/s² and a velocity of 24.5 m/s. How far will his boxcar travel when it meets these conditions?

a. 18.1 m

b. 20.8 m

c. 22.9 m

d. 24.5 m

Circular and Projectile Motion

If an object is moving along a curved path rather than a straight line, then the direction of the velocity vector is constantly changing. The change in direction constitutes an acceleration, regardless of whether or not the magnitude of the vector (the speed) is changing. Even if the speed isn't changing, as is frequently the case in circular motion, the change in direction means that the velocity is changing and that the object is accelerating. Since acceleration is defined as the rate of change of velocity, $a = \frac{\Delta v}{\Delta t}$, the acceleration may be visualized by drawing a vector subtraction diagram as shown below.

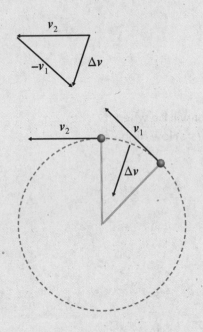

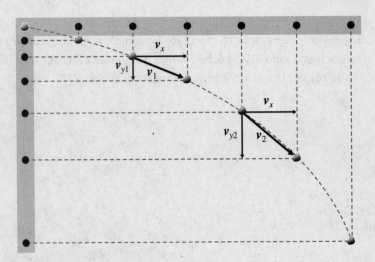

If you start by writing the equation $\Delta v = v_2 - v_1$, you can turn it into a more familiar vector addition equation by thinking of subtraction as adding the opposite of v_1 such that $\Delta v = v_2 + (-v_1)$. The diagram above shows how to visualize this calculation using the head-to-tail method. Notice that the vector Δv is clearly not zero even though the speed is constant, and that Δv points toward the center of the circle.

Develop and Use Models Draw a vector subtraction diagram above the projectile motion drawing at right showing that the change in velocity $\Delta v = v_2 - v_1$ for a projectile points downward, in the direction of the acceleration due to gravity.

Mathematical Practices:
Reason Abstractly and Quantitatively

During projectile motion, both the direction and the magnitude of the velocity vector are constantly changing. Because the horizontal and vertical components of projectile motion are independent, the arithmetic needs to be done on one component at a time. Note that there is no equation for the horizontal velocity component, v_x, since it remains constant throughout the motion.

Horizontal Equation of Motion	Vertical Equations of Motion
$\Delta x = v_x t$	$v_y = v_{iy} + gt$ and $\Delta y = v_{iy}t + \frac{1}{2}gt^2$
$\Delta x =$ horizontal displacement component	$v_y =$ vertical velocity component
$v_x =$ horizontal velocity component	$v_{iy} =$ initial vertical velocity component
	$\Delta y =$ vertical displacement component

In projectile motion problems, you often need to use the given information with an equation for one component to generate a value for the time an object has been moving, and then use that time in an equation for the other component to calculate the quantity of interest.

For example, you might do an experiment where a marble rolls off a table that is 0.85 m tall and hits the floor at a distance of 0.66 m from the edge of the table. You can use this information to determine the initial speed of the marble as follows.

First use the vertical position-time equation to calculate the time needed for the marble to reach the floor. Since the table is horizontal, you can assume the initial vertical velocity component is zero and solve for time:

$$\Delta y = (0 \text{ m/s})t + \frac{1}{2}gt^2 = \frac{1}{2}gt^2$$

$$t^2 = \frac{2\Delta y}{g}$$

$$t = \sqrt{\frac{2\Delta y}{g}} = \sqrt{\frac{2(-0.85 \text{ m})}{-9.8 \text{ m/s}^2}}$$

$$t = 0.42 \text{ s}$$

Then use this time in the horizontal position-time equation to solve for the horizontal velocity:

$$\Delta x = v_x t$$

$$v_x = \frac{\Delta x}{t} = \frac{0.66 \text{ m}}{0.42 \text{ s}} = 1.6 \text{ m/s}$$

3-Dimensional Review

1. DCI Forces and Motion A 14 kg boulder is pushed off a cliff with velocity $v = (14.0 \text{ m/s})\hat{x} + (2.0 \text{ m/s})\hat{y}$. Will the object experience a larger vertical or horizontal acceleration? Explain your answer.

_____

_____

_____

2. SEP Analyzing and Interpreting Data A golfer hits a ball into the air with initial velocity $v = v_x + v_y$.

a. Is the horizontal motion of the golf ball uniform? Explain your answer.

_____

_____

b. Is the vertical motion of the ball uniform? Explain your answer.

_____

_____

c. Fill in the position vs. time, velocity vs. time, and acceleration vs. time graphs for the horizontal and vertical motion of the golf ball.

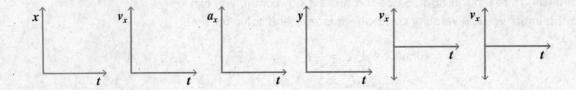

3. CCC Cause and Effect A projectile is shoved horizontally off a cliff. Which of the following would cause the projectile to have a farther horizontal displacement before hitting the ground?

a. a greater initial horizontal velocity

b. a greater initial vertical velocity

c. a greater projectile mass

d. a shorter cliff

Skills Practice

4. A professional football punter kicks a football with an initial velocity $v = (14.0 \text{ m/s})\hat{x} + (21.0 \text{ m/s})\hat{y}$. How long the football stays in the air is known as the hang time. Determine the hang time, as well as the horizontal and maximum vertical displacements.

5. A professional golfer hits a ball with an initial velocity $v = (19.0 \text{ m/s})\hat{x} + (26.0 \text{ m/s})\hat{y}$. How long the golf ball stays in the air is known as the hang time. Determine the hang time, as well as the horizontal and maximum vertical displacements.

6. A professional football punter kicks a football with an initial velocity $v = (16.0 \text{ m/s})\hat{x} + (23.0 \text{ m/s})\hat{y}$. Determine the horizontal and maximum vertical displacements.

a. $\Delta x = 37.6$ m, $\Delta y = 29.8$ m

b. $\Delta x = 37.6$ m, $\Delta y = 39.5$ m

c. $\Delta x = 75.0$ m, $\Delta y = 27.0$ m

d. $\Delta x = 75.0$ m, $\Delta y = 39.5$ m

Force, Mass, and Acceleration

Newton's laws explain the conditions needed to change the motion of an object.

The first law states that objects have inertia. That is, an object remains at rest or in uniform, straight-line motion until some action changes its motion. Mass is the measure of an object's rest inertia.

Newton's second law states that the acceleration of an object depends on the mass of the object and the net force acting on it. Objects with more mass, or inertia, require more force for the same acceleration.

Newton's Second Law of Motion (Acceleration)
$\Sigma F = ma$
ΣF = net force m = mass a = acceleration

Newton's third law states that the interaction between two objects can be represented by two forces having equal magnitude but opposite directions. These two forces are referred to as a "third-law force pair."

The vector arrows in the diagram, which are drawn to scale, model the magnitude and direction of several third-law force pairs. For example, the force of the person's hand on the cart (F_{HC}) and the force of the cart on the person's hand (F_{CH}) are a third-law pair. Notice that these forces do not act on the same object.

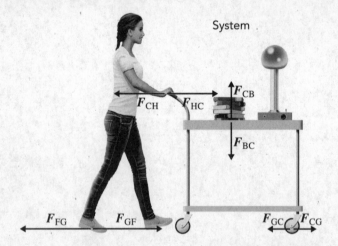

When analyzing motion scenarios, it is important to distinguish between forces that are internal and external to a system. Only external forces cause acceleration.

Use Models Circle the forces that accelerate the cart.

Do any of the forces that you circled form a third-law pair?

_____

_____

Mathematical Practices: Model with Mathematics

Applying Newton's second law to solve motion problems requires evaluating a given situation to distinguish what forces contribute to the acceleration of an object and then representing those forces symbolically in a free-body diagram.

Problem:

A 1500 kg hovercraft accelerates at 5 m/s². If the water provides 58 N of frictional force, what is the magnitude of the force that propels the hovercraft forward?

Solution:

There are internal and external forces acting in the hovercraft system. One set of internal forces include those involving the engine and the fan (not shown). Only external forces acting on the hovercraft are included in the free body diagram because they will contribute to the acceleration of the hovercraft.

Free body diagram
for the hovercraft

F_{WH} F_{AH}

The free-body diagram is useful when writing an equation for the net force (ΣF). For the hovercraft system, the net force equation is:

$$\Sigma F = F_{AH} - F_{WH}$$

where F_{AH} is the force of the air on the hovercraft and F_{WH} is the force of the water on the hovercraft. Once the net force equation is complete, it may be substituted into the second law equation.

$$\Sigma F = F_{AH} - F_{WH} = ma$$

Solve for F_{AH}.

$$F_{AH} = ma + F_{WH} = 1500 \text{ kg}(5 \text{ m/s}^2) + 58 \text{ N} = 7558 \text{ N}$$

3-Dimensional Review

1. DCI Forces and Motion The table shows the mass and net force of two cars moving down the same road. Without performing any calculations, which car will experience a greater acceleration? Explain your answer using Newton's laws.

Car	Mass (kg)	Net Force (N)
A	800 kg	400 N
B	300 kg	300 N

_____

_____

_____

2. SEP Analyzing and Interpreting Data The free-body diagram of forces on a cart that is moving right are shown in the image.

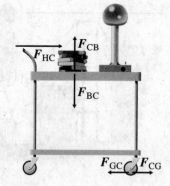

  a. Are the forces F_{CB} and F_{BC} examples of a third-law pair? Explain why or why not.

  _____

  _____

  _____

  b. Write an equation for the net force of the cart system based on the free-body diagram: _____

  c. If the force F_{HC} was removed, describe the motion of the cart. Include the direction of the motion and acceleration.

  _____

3. CCC Cause and Effect A ball is kicked to the right. The ball hits a wall and bounces backwards. According to Newton's first law, why does the ball change direction when it hits the wall? Choose the best answer.

  a. The ball experiences a non-zero net force.

  b. The ball experiences a net force of zero.

  c. The ball experiences a non-zero net force downwards.

  d. The ball experiences a non-zero net force left.

Skills Practice

4. Three forces are pushing on a box. The free-body diagram is shown. If the sum of F_{1B} and F_{2B} is equal to F_{3B}, will the box experience a change in momentum? Explain your reasoning using a force-acceleration equation and Newton's laws.

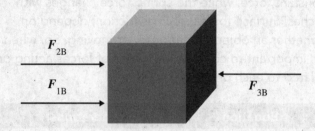

_____

_____

_____

_____

_____

5. A battery-powered lawn mower has a mass of 25.0 kg. If a student pushes the lawn mower with 15.5 N of force, the lawn mower's motor provides a force of 20.0 N, and the grass provides a resistance force of 3.00 N, what is the net force and acceleration of the lawn mower?

6. A battery-powered lawn mower has a mass of 49.0 kg. If the net external force on the lawnmower, including both your push and any resistance, is 28.0 N (about 6.3 pounds), then what will be the magnitude of the mower's acceleration?

a. $a = 0.13$ m/s^2

b. $a = 2.9$ m/s^2

c. $a = 2.0$ m/s^2

d. $a = 0.57$ m/s^2

Types of Forces

There are several types of forces and they vary in their characteristics. The force due to gravity or weight is a constant force, while the spring force changes with the distance that a spring stretches. Surface forces, such as friction, depend on the nature of the surface and whether an object is stationary or moving. So, when solving net force problems, it is important to consider the types of forces acting on an object and the equations related to each one.

Force Type	Equation	Considerations
Weight (F_{EM}) F_{EM} = force of Earth on mass	$F_{EM} = W = mg$	Weight always pulls straight down.
Spring force (F_{SO}) F_{SO} = force of spring on object	$F_{SO} = -k\Delta L$	The spring constant, k, will vary for different springs.
Tension force	—	Tension always works against the stretch direction.
Normal force	—	The normal is always perpendicular to a surface.
Static friction	$f \leq \mu_s N$	Each material will have a unique coefficient of friction, μ. Generally, $\mu_s > \mu_k$.
Kinetic friction	$f = \mu_k N$	

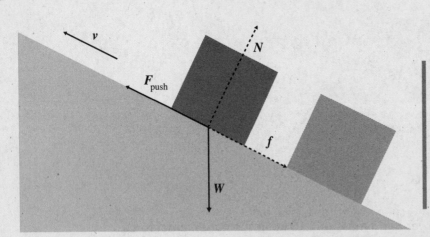

The box is being pushed up the ramp in this system. There are four forces acting on the box. Contact forces include the push, the normal force from the surface, and friction from the ramp. Weight is a non-contact force pulling straight down on the box.

Apply Mathematical Concepts What force equations are needed to solve for the acceleration of the box?

_____

Mathematical Practices: Make Sense of Problems

Understanding the different types of force helps you make sense of two-dimensional force problems.

Problem: A skier's acceleration down a 40° slope is 8 m/s². If the skier has a mass of 70 kg, what frictional force is the skier experiencing from the ground?

Step 1. Draw vectors for all noncontact forces acting on the object.

- **Weight** pulls down on the skier.

Step 2. Draw force vectors for contact forces on the object.

- The ground exerts a **normal** on the skier.
- There is **friction** from the snow and ground.

Step 3. Draw a free body diagram.

- Each force acting on the skier is represented with a vector arrow.

- The weight vector can be split into perpendicular and parallel components.

Step 4. Write force equations for each direction.

Perpendicular to the ground:

- The weight perpendicular and the normal are equal and opposite, so they cancel out.

$$N + W_{perpendicular} = 0 \text{ N}$$

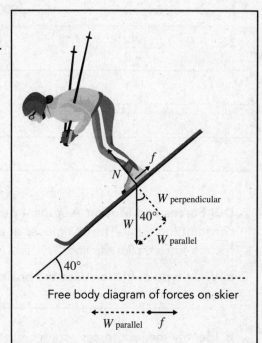

Free body diagram of forces on skier

Parallel to the ground:

- The only forces acting on the skier are the weight parallel and the friction force.

$$\Sigma F = f - W_{parallel}$$

- Recall that $W = mg$.

- The $W_{parallel}$ can be found using trigonometry.

$$W_{parallel} = W \sin\theta = mg \sin\theta$$
$$\text{So, } \Sigma F = f - mg \sin\theta$$

Step 5. Use equations to solve for the answer.

$$\Sigma F = ma$$
$$f - mg \sin\theta = ma = 70 \text{ kg} (8 \text{ m/s}^2)$$
$$f - mg \sin\theta = 560 \text{ N}$$
$$f = 560 \text{ N} + mg \sin\theta$$
$$f = 560 \text{ N} + 70 \text{ kg} (9.8 \text{ m/s}^2)(\sin 40°)$$
$$f = 1071 \text{ N}$$

3-Dimensional Review

1. **SEP Analyzing and Interpreting Data** The table shows the mass and acceleration of two elevators, each on a cable. Without performing any calculations, which cable will experience a greater tension as the elevators move? Explain your answer using force equations and Newton's laws.

Elevator	Mass (kg)	Acceleration (m/s^2)
A	800 kg	1.2 m/s^2
B	900 kg	–0.9 m/s^2

\
\
\
\

2. **DCI Forces and Motion** A student pushes a 6.0-kg box to the right with a constant force F_{SB}. The box moves at a constant velocity. The box experiences a friction force f from the floor.

   a. What type of friction does the box experience? Explain your reasoning.

   \

   b. Identify the four forces acting on the box.

   \

   c. Compare the magnitude and direction of the pair of forces F_g and N and the pair of forces F_{SB} and f.

   \
   \

3. **CCC Cause and Effect** An ideal spring is hung vertically with a mass. The spring's length at rest is 0.15 m. Which is true?

   a. The spring constant increases when the mass is added.

   b. At 0.15 m, the force of the spring on the mass is greater than gravity.

   c. If the same mass is placed on a vertical spring with a greater spring constant, the spring will stretch a lesser distance.

   d. If the same mass is placed on a vertical spring with a greater spring constant, the spring will stretch a greater distance.

Skills Practice

4. In an amusement park ride called the rotor, riders stick to the wall of a spinning cylinder. During the ride, the floor drops from beneath them, but they do not fall.

Draw and label the free-body diagram of a rider on the amusement park ride after the floor drops from beneath them.

5. A student is pulling a sled in the snow with constant velocity using a rope held at an angle. The sled's mass is 8.50 kg. The coefficient of friction between the snow and sled is 0.200. Write the tension in the rope in component form and determine its magnitude.

6. You are handed a spring that is 0.500 m long. You hang the spring from a hook on the ceiling and then attach a 0.550-kg mass to the other end of the spring. You measure the stretched spring length to be 0.850 m. Determine the change in the spring's length and the spring constant.

a. $\Delta L = 0.35$ m $k = 12.3$ N/m

b. $\Delta L = 1.35$ m $k = 6.35$ N/m

c. $\Delta L = 0.35$ m $k = 15.4$ N/m

d. $\Delta L = 1.35$ m $k = 15.0$ N/m

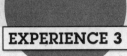
Forces on Systems

Many real-world systems involve multiple objects and forces acting in different directions. To analyze motion in these complex systems, the first step is to define what objects to include in the system. Identifying internal and external forces that act on objects in the system is next. The external forces acting determine the motion of each object. Once the system is defined, a free-body diagram and force-acceleration equation may be constructed for each object, and these will help to determine a model for the whole system.

It is also important to determine whether or not the system is in a state of equilibrium. When in dynamic equilibrium, objects move with constant velocity by inertia alone. When in static equilibrium, objects do not move. Whether in dynamic equilibrium or static equilibrium, the net force acting on the object is zero and torque is zero. Torque is the measure of how effective a force is at producing a rotation, and it is the product of the magnitude of the force and the lever arm (the distance from the force to the point of rotation).

Torque
$$\tau = r_{perp}F$$
τ = torque $\qquad$ r_{perp} = lever arm $\qquad$ F = force

The acceleration, net force, and torque for a system in equilibrium can be set equal to zero.

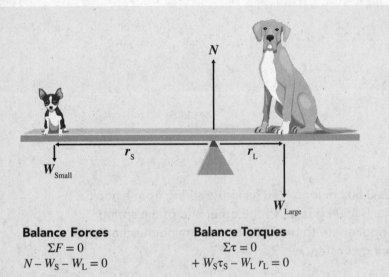

Static Equilibrium
This system is in static equilibrium. Forces sum to zero and torques sum to zero.

Balance Forces
$$\Sigma F = 0$$
$$N - W_S - W_L = 0$$

Balance Torques
$$\Sigma \tau = 0$$
$$+ W_S \tau_S - W_L \, r_L = 0$$

Note the sign convention established for the clockwise (+) and counterclockwise (−) directions.

Use Math How do the lever arm distances to each dog compare if the large dog is four (4) times more massive than the small dog? Show your math reasoning.

Mathematical Practices: Model with Mathematics

Solving motion problems for complex systems involves identifying important quantities, mapping their relationships using diagrams, and writing force-acceleration equations. Important quantities include masses, forces, and torques. They might also include quantities that appear in the equations for various force types, such as the coefficient of friction for a material, the acceleration due to gravity, or a spring constant.

Mapping relationships involves constructing a diagram of the entire system, then deconstructing the system by drawing a free-body diagram for each object. This process helps you determine if the system is in equilibrium or if the motion of objects is changing.

Using Mathematical Models to Represent a Pulley System

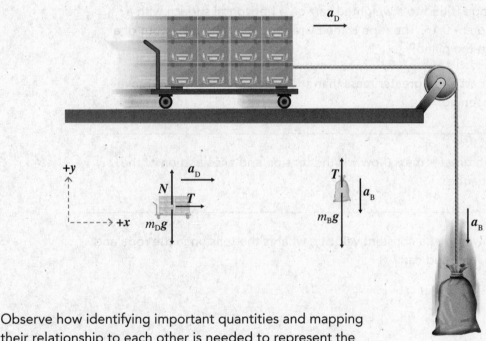

Observe how identifying important quantities and mapping their relationship to each other is needed to represent the pulley system. Important quantities in the pulley system include:

- Mass of the furniture dolly (m_D)

- Mass of the bag (m_B)

- Acceleration due to gravity (g)

- Tension (T)

- Normal on the furniture dolly (N)

The relationships among these quantities is understood by using them to label forces in free-body diagrams. The diagrams help you write specific force-acceleration equations for each object, one for each direction of motion (x and y). Such equations can help you answer questions about the pulley system.

3-Dimensional Review

1. SEP Analyzing and Interpreting Data A meter stick is balanced at its center. The table shows the weight and distance from the center of two weights on the meter stick. Will it be in static equilibrium? Explain your reasoning using torque.

Weight	Weight (N)	Distance to Center (m)
A	0.50 N	0.2 m to the right
B	0.30 N	0.4 m to the left

_____

_____

2. DCI Forces and Motion A rope and pulley are used to lower a piano with a mass of 450.0 kg. The rope is tied to a weighted cart on a horizontal surface with a coefficient of friction of 0.16. The rope is then wrapped over the pulley out of a window and tied to the piano.

a. If the weighted cart has a greater mass than the piano, will the system move? Explain your reasoning.

_____

b. If the piano has a greater mass, how will the tension and acceleration of the weighted cart change?

_____

c. If the piano is lowered at a constant velocity, what is the tension in the rope and the mass of the weighted cart?

3. CCC Cause and Effect A meter stick is balanced at its center using a support. Two weights of different masses are hung on either side. The meter stick stays balanced and does not move. Which of the following statements accurately describes what is happening?

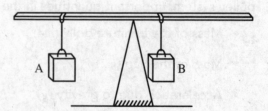

a. Weight A provides a greater torque.

b. Weight B has a greater mass.

c. Both weights are the same mass as the stick is in static equilibrium.

d. Both weights provide the same torque as the stick is in static equilibrium.

Skills Practice

4. A meter stick is balanced at its center using a support. A 0.45-N weight is hung on the meter stick a distance 0.30 m from the center to the right. Where should you place a 0.20-N weight such that the meter stick is in static equilibrium?

5. An Atwood machine is a mechanical system consisting of two objects connected via a rope over a pulley. Suppose two objects, A and B, are connected by a rope. The rope is hung over a frictionless pulley with an object hanging on either side. The system is allowed to move freely. Object A has a mass of 21.0 kg and object B has a mass of 15.0 kg. If object A is released from rest, determine the magnitude of the acceleration and tension for object B. Assume the rope and pulley are massless.

6. A meter stick is balanced at its center using a support. Two weights of unknown mass are hung on either side of the meter stick, as shown in the image. Which of the following statements accurately describes the relationship between the two weights?

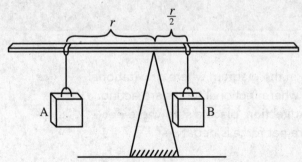

a. $W_A = W_B$

b. $W_A = 2W_B$

c. $W_A = \frac{1}{2}W_B$

d. $W_A = \frac{1}{3}W_B$

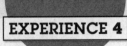
Earth's Surface Forces

Constructive and destructive forces drive processes that shape the surface of Earth. These forces operate at different scales, and the changes they cause can be gradual or catastrophic. Large-scale forces include the mechanical forces that shift tectonic plates or the force due to pressure that propels magma up to the mouth of a volcano. Small-scale forces include the electric forces between water molecules and minerals in rock. These tiny forces break apart rock over time in a process called weathering.

The forces acting at different scales often work together to change Earth's surface. For example, gravity pulls rainwater and loose rocks down mountain slopes. This causes frictional forces between the water, rocks, and ground. The frictional forces work together with electric forces to cause weathering.

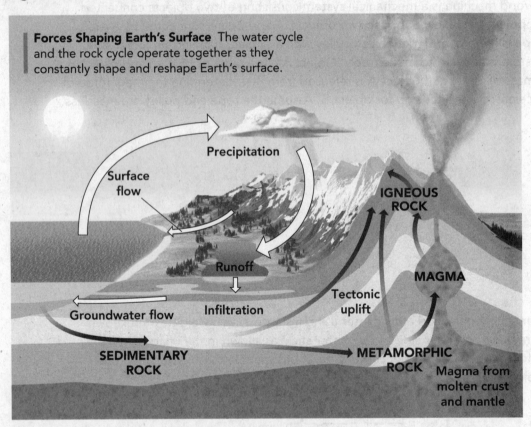

Forces Shaping Earth's Surface The water cycle and the rock cycle operate together as they constantly shape and reshape Earth's surface.

Interpret Data Circle a location in the diagram where gravitational forces are acting. Box a location where frictional forces are acting. Assuming that up is the positive direction, place a star where net force is positive. Place an X where net force is negative.

Science Practices: Engaging in Argument from Evidence

Scientists use patterns they observe in Earth systems to identify cause-effect relationships related to processes that shape the surface of Earth. Some patterns are visible by simply observing land or ocean characteristics. Other patterns are revealed by analyzing data. Explanations of how forces affect matter provide the reasoning that links patterns in Earth system data with claims about how Earth's surface changes over time.

The diagrams below show how forces along the coast can smooth jagged coastlines.

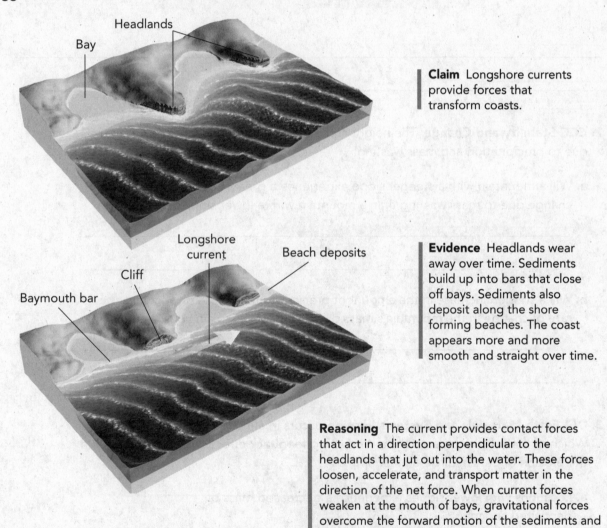

Claim Longshore currents provide forces that transform coasts.

Evidence Headlands wear away over time. Sediments build up into bars that close off bays. Sediments also deposit along the shore forming beaches. The coast appears more and more smooth and straight over time.

Reasoning The current provides contact forces that act in a direction perpendicular to the headlands that jut out into the water. These forces loosen, accelerate, and transport matter in the direction of the net force. When current forces weaken at the mouth of bays, gravitational forces overcome the forward motion of the sediments and they fall to form beach deposits.

This claim-evidence-reasoning example shows how the relationship between net force, mass, and acceleration may be used to support arguments about changes in Earth systems. In this example, contact forces between wind and ocean water cause currents that push (F_{net}) sand and rocks (*mass*), displacing them from where they are at rest so that they move along the shore (*acceleration*).

3-Dimensional Review

1. SEP Developing and Using Models Compare the forces that shape the desert landscape at A and B. Describe how destructive and constructive processes produce the shape of the landscape.

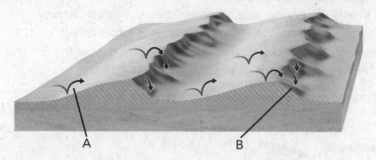

_____

_____

2. CCC Stability and Change The height and mass of a mountain is in constant flux due to precipitation and mass wasting.

a. Will a mountain with a steeper slope experience a greater or lesser rate of change due to mass wasting than a mountain with a lower slope? Explain.

_____

_____

b. Will a sudden increase in the amount of precipitation increase or decrease the rate of change in the mountain's mass due to erosion? Explain your reasoning.

_____

_____

3. DCI Earth Materials and Systems Erosion occurs in almost all of Earth's systems. Which of the following describes a reinforcing feedback effect due to an increase in the erosion of Earth? Circle all that apply.

a. Locations with lower slopes experience a decreased mass of deposited sediments.

b. Increased sedimentation compacts and cements particles into new rock.

c. A glacier's mass decreases as sediment is deposited in the terminal moraine.

d. Mountain mass is reduced, and isostatic pressure becomes imbalanced causing the crust to rebound upward.

e. Beach deposits decrease as headlands and coastlines become more jagged.

Skills Practice

4. A student collects data from the Colorado river to create the data table shown.

Date	Discharge m³/s	Stream Flow m/s
09/10/2020	102	1116
07/21/2020	68.8	20.97
07/01/2020	129.7	1490
06/09/2020	291.66	3078

Based on the data, identify the connection between streamflow and discharge rate by describing the relationship between erosion and the amount of sediment.

_____

_____

_____

5. A mountain range has evidence of metamorphic rocks exposed at the surface. How can the evidence of metamorphic rocks be used to reason that isostasy occurred in the continental crust based on the claim—evidence—reasoning model?

_____

_____

6. The Scablands in Washington are large areas of erosion due to immense flooding. A student claims the flooding of the Scablands is due to erosion and melting of glaciers which increased the amount of water until it overwhelmed the dams. Using the claim and map shown, create a claim—evidence—reasoning model.

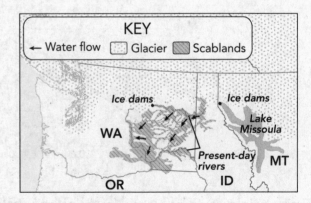

_____

_____

_____

_____

Universal Gravitation

Earth's gravitational field is essentially uniform (constant in both magnitude and direction) close to Earth's surface, but it weakens exponentially with distance according to this formula:

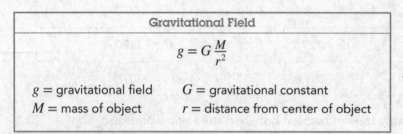

Gravitational Field
$$g = G\frac{M}{r^2}$$

g = gravitational field G = gravitational constant
M = mass of object r = distance from center of object

In vector models of fields, the weakening of the field is revealed by diverging field lines. In a graph of field strength versus distance from the center, it is revealed by an exponential curve with a negative slope. At two times the radius of Earth, the gravitational field weakens to one-fourth its original strength. Since the acceleration due to gravity depends on the field strength, the inverse-square relationship affects the acceleration of satellites at different distances from Earth's surface.

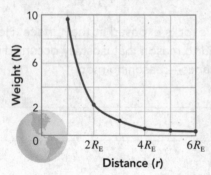

The first graph shows the weight of a 1-kg mass at different distances from Earth's center. On Earth's surface, a 1-kg mass weighs 9.8 N. As the mass moves farther away from Earth's surface, the force of gravity on the mass, which is its weight, decreases.

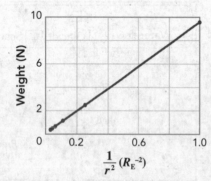

The second graph shows that weight is proportional to $\frac{1}{r^2}$. The inverse square proportionality occurs when any quantity radiates outward from a source in all directions.

Similar graphs could be plotted for the electric field around a charged object or the intensity of light or sound emanating from a point source.

Use Math Suppose scientists launch two satellites. One satellite is $1.1R_E$ from Earth and the other is $1.2R_E$ from Earth. Which satellite has the greater acceleration due to gravity as it orbits Earth? By what factor?

_____

_____

Mathematical Practices: Attend to Precision

Scientists and engineers must attend to precision when they report numerical quantities because precise quantities are need to make reliable predictions or to design dependable solutions. The precision of a measured or calculated value can be understood as how close the measured or calculated value is to the actual value.

Consider how an engineer might need to attend to precision when estimating the force of gravity on a satellite orbiting Earth using Newton's law of universal gravitation.

Newton's Law of Universal Gravitation

$$F = G\frac{m_1 m_2}{r_{12}^2}$$

G = gravitational constant = 6.674×10^{-11} m³/(kg · s²)

m_1 = mass 1 m_2 = mass 2

r_{12} = distance between centers of mass 1 and mass 2

The precision of any value calculated using this (or any) equation depends on the **least** precise measurement included in the calculation. The precision of a quantity is communicated through the use of significant figures.

Sample Problem

The average distance between the International Space Station (ISS) and Earth is 400 km (400,000 m). The mass of Earth is 5.97×10^{24} kg and the mass of the space station is 419,725 kg. What is the average force exerted by Earth on the space station?

Step 1 Use knowns to solve for the unknown

$$F_{ES} = G\frac{m_E m_S}{r_{ES}^2} = 6.67 \times 10^{-11} \text{ m}^3/(\text{kg·s}^2) \times \left(\frac{5.97 \times 10^{24} \text{ kg} \times 419,725 \text{ kg}}{(400,000 \text{ m})^2} \right)$$

$$F_{ES} = 1,044,587,870 \text{ N}$$

Step 2 Consider significant figures

The least precise quantity in this calculation is the distance between Earth and the space station, r_{ES}. The value given for r_{ES} includes one significant figure. Therefore, the answer should only include one significant figure.

$$F_{ES} = 1,000,000,000 \text{ N (or } 1 \times 10^9 \text{ N)}$$

The exact gravitational force acting on the space station at a specific point in its orbit cannot be calculated with the information given. The distance between the space station and Earth varies along the space station's elliptical orbit, so the average distance is provided. Depending on the range of values used to find this average, the average could be very accurate (small range) or not very accurate (large range). This imprecision is reflected in the reported answer.

If a precise distance between the ISS and Earth is known, such as 403 km, then your final answer can be reported with more precision. Since 403 km has 3 significant figures, the answer can be reported as $F_{ES} = 1.04 \times 10^9$ N.

3-Dimensional Review

1. DCI Types of Interactions Describe, in your own words, how Newton's law of universal gravitation relates gravitational force to mass and distance.

_____

_____

_____

2. SEP Using Mathematical and Computational Thinking Answer the following questions about Newton's law of universal gravitation.

    a. Assuming the distance between two objects does not change, what would cause a decrease in the gravitational force between them?

    _____

    _____

    b. You find the gravitational force between two objects to be 1200 N. If you double the distance between the objects, what will be the resulting gravitational force between them? Explain your reasoning.

    _____

    _____

    _____

    c. Assuming the mass of two objects does not change, what would cause a decrease in the gravitational force between them?

    _____

    _____

3. CCC Patterns Which of the following is a pattern of the gravitational force between two masses? Circle all that apply.

    a. As the masses increase, the magnitude of the force increases.

    b. The larger mass experiences a force equal and opposite the force of the smaller mass.

    c. As the distance increases, the magnitude of the force increases.

    d. As the masses increase, the distance between them increases.

Skills Practice

4. Calculate the force exerted by Mars on its moon, Phobos, and the force exerted by Phobos on Mars. The mass of Mars is 6.4×10^{23} kg and the mass of Phobos is 1.06×10^{16} kg. The distance between Mars' and Phobos' centers of mass is 9.38×10^{6} m. Express your answers as vectors.

5. Calculate the force exerted by Jupiter on its moon Ganymede and the force exerted by Ganymede on Jupiter. The mass of Jupiter is about 1.9×10^{27} kg, and the mass of Ganymede is about 1.5×10^{23} kg. The distance between Jupiter's and Ganymede's centers of mass is 1.1×10^{6} km. Express your answers as vectors.

6. Calculate the force exerted by the moon, Triton, on its planet Neptune. The mass of Neptune is about 1.02×10^{26} kg, and the mass of Triton is about 2.14×10^{22} kg. The distance between their centers of mass is 3.55×10^{5} km. Choose the direction toward Triton's center of mass as the positive x-direction.

a. $(4.10 \times 10^{32} \text{ N})\hat{x}$

b. $(-4.10 \times 10^{32} \text{ N})\hat{x}$

c. $(1.16 \times 10^{27} \text{ N})\hat{x}$

d. $(-1.16 \times 10^{27} \text{ N})\hat{x}$

Orbital Motion

Centripetal, or center-directed, forces are required for orbital motion. An object in orbital motion has linear velocity (v), angular velocity (ω), and centripetal acceleration (a_c). It also has a period of orbit (T), which is the time to complete one revolution. Orbital motion is described by these formulas:

Period and Centripetal Acceleration

$$T = \frac{C}{v} = \frac{2\pi r}{v} = \frac{2\pi}{\omega} \qquad\qquad a_c = \frac{v^2}{r} = \omega^2 r$$

T = period
C = circumference
ω = angular velocity = $\frac{v}{r}$

v = velocity
r = radius
a_c = centripetal acceleration

When an object is orbiting a planet, such as when a satellite orbits Earth, the period and velocity of the object depends on its distance from the planet's surface.

Orbital Velocity

$$v = \left(\frac{GM_E}{r}\right)^{\frac{1}{2}}$$

v = orbital velocity
G = gravitational constant = 6.674×10^{-11} m³/(kg · s²)
M_E = mass of Earth = 5.972×10^{24} kg
r = radius of satellite orbit, measured from the center of Earth (m)

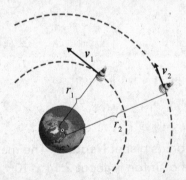

Different Orbits Satellites at different distances from Earth's center travel at different speeds. The speed decreases as the inverse of $r^{1/2}$.

Orbital motion equations can be used to represent the motion of moons around planets or other planets around the sun.

Apply Mathematical Concepts According to the equation for orbital velocity, does Mercury orbit the sun at a higher velocity than Jupiter because Mercury is less massive, because it is closer to the sun, or for both of these reasons?

Mathematical Practices: Make Use of Structure

Mathematically proficient students can use the fact that some quantities may be represented by more than one equation in order to develop solution strategies. Equations for the same quantity can be set equal to each other to solve for an unknown.

Orbital velocity (v) may be represented by two equations. Setting these equations equal to each other allows you to solve for the radius (r) or the period of the orbit (T).

$$v = \left(\frac{GM_E}{r}\right)^{\frac{1}{2}} = \frac{2\pi r}{T}$$

Sample Problem

Europa is a moon orbiting Jupiter. Astronomers have determined that Europa is approximately 617,000 km from Jupiter, which has a mass of 1.898×10^{27} kg. What is the orbital period (in hours) of Europa around Jupiter?

Step 1 Identify knowns and unknowns

Knowns
G = gravitational constant
$\quad = 6.67 \times 10^{-11}$ Nm^2 kg^{-2}
M_J = mass of Jupiter
$\quad = 1.898 \times 10^{27}$ kg
r = radius of orbit
$\quad = 617,000$ km (or 6.17×10^8 m)

Unknown
T = period

Step 2 Use the equations for orbital velocity to solve for *T*

$$\left(\frac{GM_J}{r}\right)^{\frac{1}{2}} = \frac{2\pi r}{T}, \text{ so } \ldots T = 2\pi\left(\frac{r^3}{GM_J}\right)^{\frac{1}{2}}$$

Step 3 Solve

$$T = 2\pi\left(\frac{r^3}{GM_J}\right)^{\frac{1}{2}} = 2\pi\left(\frac{(6.709 \times 10^8 \text{ m})^3}{(6.67 \times 10^{-11} \text{ Nm}^2 \text{ kg}^{-2})(1.898 \times 10^{27} \text{ kg})}\right)^{\frac{1}{2}}$$

$T = 306,871$ seconds or 85.2 hours

3-Dimensional Review

1. DCI Earth and the Solar System If Newton's first law states that an object will travel in a straight line unless impacted by an outside force, why do satellites orbit Earth in a circular manner?

_____

_____

_____

2. SEP Using Mathematical and Computational Thinking

a. According to the orbital velocity equation, for a satellite to orbit at a higher velocity, what must happen?

_____

_____

b. How is the period of a satellite related to its orbital velocity? What does this mean?

_____

_____

c. Can you use the orbital velocity equation for other planets? Explain your answer.

_____

_____

3. CCC Scale, Proportion, and Quantity Which satellite would have the farthest orbit?

a. a satellite above Jupiter in geosynchronous orbit

b. a satellite orbiting Jupiter once every 24 Earth hours

c. a GPS satellite above Jupiter orbiting once every 12 Earth hours

d. a satellite orbiting Jupiter once every 6 Earth hours

Skills Practice

4. NASA's Aqua satellite orbits Earth every 99 minutes. Calculate how far above Earth's surface Aqua's orbit must be.

5. The average weather satellite orbits Earth about once every 23.93 hours. Calculate the radius of such an orbit.

6. A satellite needs to orbit Earth at a height of 380 km above Earth's surface. Calculate the orbital period of the satellite.

a. 4.62×10^3 s

b. 5.52×10^3 s

c. 8.18×10^4 s

d. 9.30×10^{14} s

Kepler's Laws

The orbits of the planets around the sun are elliptical, not circular. Kepler's three laws use mathematics to describe the elliptical motion of the planets and other objects around the sun.

- **Kepler's first law** states that planets orbit the sun in elliptical paths with the sun located at one focus of the ellipse.

- **Kepler's second law** states that a line drawn from the sun to a planet will sweep out equal areas of space in equal periods of time. This means that a planet orbiting the sun travels faster when it is closer to the sun.

- **Kepler's third law** states that the orbital period depends on the radius of a circular orbit or the semimajor axis of an ellipse.

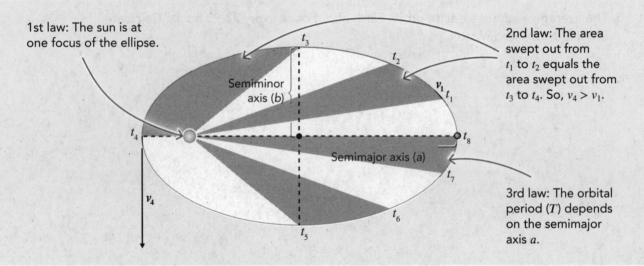

1st law: The sun is at one focus of the ellipse.

Semiminor axis (b)

Semimajor axis (a)

2nd law: The area swept out from t_1 to t_2 equals the area swept out from t_3 to t_4. So, $v_4 > v_1$.

3rd law: The orbital period (T) depends on the semimajor axis a.

The formulas connected to each of Kepler's laws are presented below.

First Law	Second Law	Third Law
Ellipse equation $$\frac{x^2}{a^2} + \frac{y^2}{b^2} = 1$$ **Focus of an ellipse (c)** $$c = \sqrt{|a^2 - b^2|}$$	**Instantaneous velocity of an object in an elliptical orbit** $$v = \left(GM\left(\frac{2}{r} - \frac{1}{a}\right)\right)^{\frac{1}{2}}$$	**Period of an elliptical orbit** $$T^2 = 4\pi^2\left(\frac{a^3}{GM}\right)$$
a = semimajor axis b = semiminor axis	v = instantaneous velocity r = distance between 2 bodies	T = period of the orbit G = gravitational constant M = mass of the orbited object

Reason Quantitatively Circle the word that correctly completes this sentence:

Referring to the diagram, as the semimajor axis of an elliptical orbit increases, the difference between the magnitudes of v_1 and v_4 _____.

increases   decreases   remains constant

Mathematical Practices: Model with Mathematics

Using scaled diagrams to model orbital motion is useful for observing the eccentricity of an orbit, which is the degree to which an orbit is flattened into an elliptical shape.

Drawing a Model of an Elliptical Orbit

Suppose the perigee distance (the shortest distance) of a moon as it orbits a planet is 0.8 million km and its apogee distance (the longest distance) is 13.2 million km. This moon's orbit has a high eccentricity. Follow these steps to draw a model of this system:

1. Calculate the major axis distance for the elliptical orbit by finding the sum of the perigee and apogee distances.

2. Establish a distance scale for the model. In the graph model for this system, 1 tick mark = 1 cm = 10 million kilometers.

3. Mark each vertex on the graph using the to-scale major axis distance. Since the major axis of this moon's orbit is 140 million km, the to-scale major axis distance is 14 cm. It extends from the vertex at $x = -7$ to the vertex at $x = +7$.

4. Use the to-scale perigee distance to mark each focus of the ellipse. In this system, the perigee distance is 8 million km, or 0.8 cm. On the graph, one focus is at $x = -6.2$ and the other is at $x = +6.2$.

5. Cut a string that matches the to-scale major axis (14 cm) and pin each end of the string to a focus on the graph. Use a pencil to draw an ellipse around the two foci, keeping the string taut as you trace the ellipse.

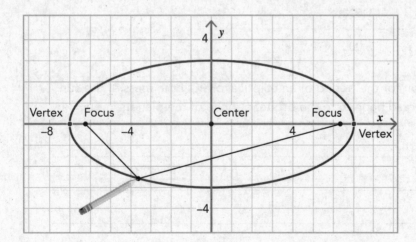

The to-scale model can be used with orbital motion equations to estimate other quantities associated with the moon's motion, such as the instantaneous velocity (v) when the moon is at perigee or apogee.

3-Dimensional Review

1. DCI Earth and the Solar System Using Kepler's Laws, explain why Mars has a shorter year than Neptune.

_____

_____

_____

2. SEP Using Mathematical and Computational Thinking

    a. According to Kepler's third law, what type of relationship exists between the semimajor axis and the orbital period?

    _____

    _____

    _____

    b. Use the given values for semimajor axis length in AU to fill in the period values in years for the rest of the table for different orbits around the sun.

a	T
2.000	2.828
3.000	
5.000	
8.000	

    c. Based on the equation for the period of an elliptical orbit, if the mass of the sun were smaller, what would happen to the orbital periods of the planets in our solar system?

    _____

    _____

    _____

3. CCC Scale, Proportion, and Quantity If the average orbital velocity is $\frac{2\pi r}{T}$, which of the following planets will have a slower orbital velocity than Earth? Circle all that apply.

    a. Mercury   **b.** Jupiter

    c. Venus   **d.** Saturn

Skills Practice

4. Mars has an orbital period of about 687 Earth days. Find the semimajor axis of its orbit. Remember that the mass of the sun is 1.988×10^{30} kg.

5. Mercury has an orbital period of about 88 Earth days. Find the semimajor axis of its orbit. Remember that the mass of the sun is 1.988×10^{30} kg.

6. Neptune has an orbital period of about 60,200 Earth days. Find the semimajor axis of its orbit. Remember that the mass of the sun is 1.988×10^{30} kg.

a. 4.496×10^{12} m

b. 8.823×10^{19} m

c. 1.754×10^{28} m

d. 9.081×10^{37} m

Coulomb's Law

According to Coulomb's Law, the electric force between two charged objects depends on the inverse square of the distance between them and the quantity of charge on each object.

A free body diagram with a defined coordinate system can be used to represent the forces acting on each charged object in a system.

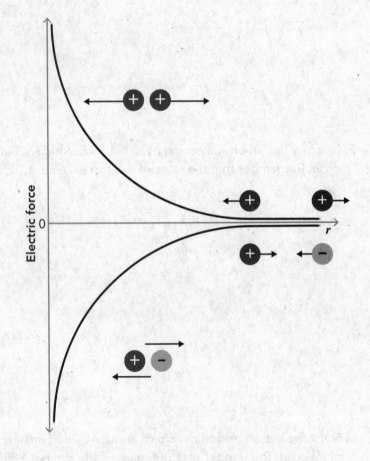

Coulomb's Law
$$F_e = k_e \frac{q_1 q_2}{r_{12}^2}$$

F_e = magnitude of the electric force
$k_e = 8.99 \times 10^9 \text{ N} \cdot \text{m}^2/\text{C}^2$
q_1 = charge of object 1
q_2 = charge of object 2
r_{12} = distance between objects 1 and 2

Use Models What does it mean if a force is positive or negative in the diagram? Does the mathematical sign of a force relate to its strength?

_____

_____

How do the vector arrows on the diagram align with Coulomb's Law?

_____

_____

_____

Mathematical Practices: Model with Mathematics

When more than two charged objects are present in a system, each charge will experience multiple forces that combine to determine the net force. It is helpful to model these systems using free body diagrams and a consistent labeling system to distinguish forces. A coordinate system must be defined for the model in order to distinguish force directions mathematically.

In the system of charges shown below, q experiences two repulsive forces.

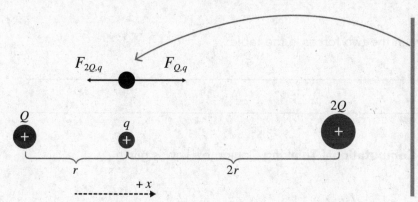

The free body diagram for q includes a vector arrow for each force. The vectors are labeled to distinguish the source of each force. $F_{2Q,q}$ means "the force of charge $2Q$ on q." The force of Q on the test charge is greater than the force of $2Q$, even though its charge magnitude is smaller. This is because $2Q$ is twice the distance from the test charge.

The coordinate system provided defines the positive direction. While both forces on q are repulsive, they act in opposite directions. This must be considered when writing the net force equation for q:

$$\Sigma F = -F_{2Q,q} + F_{Q,q}$$

The net force equation can be rewritten using Coulomb's Law:

$$\Sigma F = -k_e \frac{2Qq}{(2r)^2} + k_e \frac{Qq}{(r)^2}$$

When simplified, the equation reveals that $F_{2Q,q}$ is one-half the magnitude of $F_{Q,q}$. This is reflected in the length of the vector arrows in the free body diagram.

$$\Sigma F = -k_e \frac{Qq}{2r^2} + k_e \frac{Qq}{r^2}$$

You can simplify this equation to find the net force

$$\Sigma F = k_e \frac{Qq}{r^2}$$

The positive value indicates that the net force is directed to the right.

3-Dimensional Review

1. DCI Types of Interactions Fill in the table below comparing the two forces.

Force	Interaction (attractive or repulsive?)	Equation
	only attractive	$F_g = G\left[\frac{((m_1)(m_2))}{r^2}\right]$
Electric Force		

Describe the differences between the two forces in the table.

_____

_____

2. SEP Using Mathematics and Computational Thinking Coulomb's Law is given as follows:

$$F_E = k\left(\frac{|q_1 q_2|}{r^2}\right)$$

a. How can you describe in words the relationship between the electric force and the product of charges?_____

b. How can you describe in words the relationship between the electric force and the distance between the charges?

_____

c. What happens if you double the charges of the particles?

_____

d. What happens if you double the distance between the particles?

_____

3. CCC Patterns Which of the following is **not** a pattern you notice about electric force and gravitational force?

a. both are inversely proportional to the square of their distances

b. both rely on a relationship between two objects

c. both can lead to an attractive force

d. both can lead to a repulsive force

Skills Practice

4. Three point charges are arranged in a straight line. The charges from left to right are $q_1 = 7 \ \mu C$, $q_2 = -7 \ \mu C$, and $q_3 = 7 \ \mu C$. Charge q_1 is 12 cm from charge q_2, and charge q_3 is 12 cm from charge q_2. Sketch a picture of the situation and determine the magnitude and direction of the net electric force on charge q_1.

5. Three point charges are arranged in a straight line. The charges from left to right are $q_1 = 9 \ \mu C$, $q_2 = -8 \ \mu C$, and $q_3 = 7 \ \mu C$. Charge q_1 is 11 cm from charge q_2, and charge q_3 is 8.0 cm from charge q_2. Sketch a picture of the situation and determine the magnitude and direction of the net electric force on charge q_1.

6. Three point charges are arranged in a straight line. The charges are $q_1 = 4 \ \mu C$, $q_2 = -5 \ \mu C$, and $q_3 = 6 \ \mu C$. Charge q_1 is 3 cm from charge q_2, and charge q_3 is 3 cm from charge q_2. What is the magnitude of the net electric force on charge q_1?

a. 59.9 N

b. 200 N

c. 140 N

d. 260 N

Electric Fields

An electric field is a vector field. Each location in the field can be described by the force on a tiny positive "test" charge.

Electric Field at a Point
$$E = \frac{F}{q_{\text{test}}} = \frac{k_e |q|}{r^2}$$

F = force on the test charge q_{test} = test charge
$k_e = 8.99 \times 10^9 \text{ N} \cdot \text{m}^2/\text{C}^2$ q = object charge
r = distance between object
     and test charge

The positive test charge in the diagram experiences forces from the electric fields surrounding each negative object (E_1 and E_2). The direction of the net electric field is determined by the charges of the objects producing the field and by the coordinate system you define.

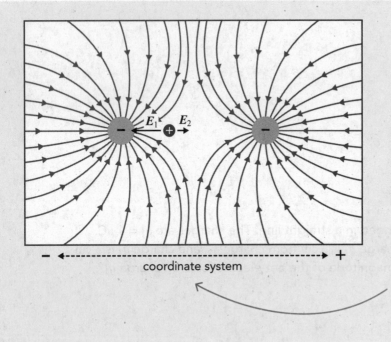

Because the test charge is closer to the charged object on the left, $E_1 > E_2$.

coordinate system

The coordinate system below the diagram establishes positive and negative directions for the system.

Apply Mathematical Concepts Based on the coordinate system shown, which equation correctly represents the strength of the electric field at the positive test charge? Circle your choice.

$E_{\text{test}} = E_1 + E_2$ $E_{\text{test}} = E_1 - E_2$ $E_{\text{test}} = -E_1 + E_2$

Mathematical Practices: Attend to Precision

Calculating accurately with the electric field equation requires careful attention to mathematical symbols and units of measure.

What strategies can you use to find an accurate magnitude and direction for the strength of the electric field at the positive test charge?

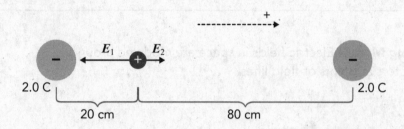

Check for unit consistency as you identify knowns and unknowns.

$q_1 = 2.0 \text{ C}$

$q_2 = 2.0 \text{ C}$

$r_1 = 20 \text{ cm} = \textbf{0.20 m}$ ⎤

$r_2 = 80 \text{ cm} = \textbf{0.80 m}$ ⎦   The distance units must be consistent. Convert cm to m.

$k_e = 8.99 \times 10^9 \text{ N} \cdot \text{m}^2/\text{C}^2$

$E_1 = ?$

$E_2 = ?$

$E_{\text{test}} = ?$

Assign mathematical signs consistently using a coordinate system.

$E_{\text{test}} = -E_1 + E_2$

$E_{\text{test}} = -\dfrac{k_e|q_1|}{r^2} + \dfrac{k_e|q_2|}{r^2}$

According to the coordinate system, E_1 is negative and E_2 is positive.

Use significant figures correctly and check answer units.

$E_{\text{test}} = -\dfrac{8.99 \times 10^9 \text{ N} \cdot \text{m}^2/\text{C}^2 \; |2.0 \text{ C}|}{(0.20 \text{ m})^2} + \dfrac{8.99 \times 10^9 \text{ N} \cdot \text{m}^2/\text{C}^2 \; |2.0 \text{ C}|}{(0.80 \text{ m})^2}$

$E_{\text{test}} = -4.2 \times 10^{11} \text{ N/C}$

The answer must include two significant figures, which is the same number of figures present in the **least** precise value in the calculation. The units N/C, or newtons per coulomb, are the units for force per charge, which makes sense for field strength.

3-Dimensional Review

1. DCI Types of Interactions How can you use fields to describe the force between two distant electric charges?

_____

_____

_____

2. SEP Developing and Using Models Electric fields in space are modeled around a charged particle using vectors at points or field lines.

    a. Based on the image above, is the charge weak or strong? Is it positive or negative? Explain your answers.

       _____

       _____

    b. Assume a second **identical** charge were to the left of this charge. What would be the value of the electric field directly between? Draw a picture of the resulting electric field.

    c. Assume a second **opposite** charge were to the left of this charge. What would the electric field look like? Draw a picture of the resulting electric field.

3. CCC Cause and Effect In a conductor, electric charges spread out across the surface. If an electric field had any component along the surface of a conductor, what would the charges do?

    a. charges would move to cancel that component

    b. charges would move to maximize that component

    c. charges would remain fixed

    d. charges would move with no specific pattern

Skills Practice

4. Two point charges are arranged in a line with point P. The point charges are $q_1 = 12 \times 10^6$ C and $q_2 = -12 \times 10^6$ C. Charge q_1 is 0.10 m to the left of charge q_2 and charge q_2 is 0.10 m to the left of point P. Sketch a picture of the situation and determine the net electric field at point P.

5. Two point charges are arranged in a line with point P. The point charges are $q_1 = 8.00 \times 10^6$ C and $q_2 = -4.00 \times 10^6$ C. Charge q_1 is 0.080 m to the left of charge q_2 and charge q_2 is 0.040 m to the left of point P. Sketch a picture of the situation and determine the net electric field at point P.

6. Two point charges are arranged in a line with point P. The point charges are $q_1 = 9 \ \mu$C and $q_2 = -3 \ \mu$C. Charge q_1 is 5 cm to the left of charge q_2 and charge q_2 is 5 cm to the left of point P. Determine the net electric field at point P.

a. -10.8 N/C

b. -2.70 N/C

c. 8.09 N/C

d. 18.9 N/C

Electric Current

While resistors connected in series can be added to find the total resistance, resistors in parallel cannot. The total resistance (or equivalent resistance) of resistors connected in parallel is lower than any of the individual resistances.

Parallel Combination of Resistors
$$\frac{1}{R_{equ}} = \frac{1}{R_1} + \frac{1}{R_2} + \frac{1}{R_3}$$
R_{equ} = equivalent resistance
R_1 = resistance of resistor 1
R_2 = resistance of resistor 2
R_3 = resistance of resistor 3

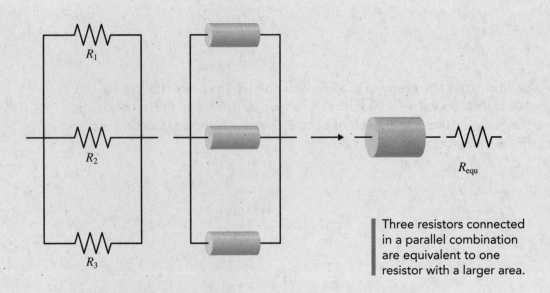

Three resistors connected in a parallel combination are equivalent to one resistor with a larger area.

Defend Your Claim Suppose the three resistors in the diagram have the following resistances: $R_1 = 220\ \Omega$, $R_2 = 100\ \Omega$, and, $R_3 = 150\ \Omega$. A student claims that the equivalent resistance is approximately 155 Ω. Is the student correct? Defend your claim with evidence.

_____

_____

_____

_____

_____

Mathematical Practices: Look for Repeated Reasoning

Complex circuits include resistors in series and in parallel. Solving for the total resistance of a complex circuit might involve calculating equivalent resistances multiple times. Locating and marking where you will repeat this step can help you develop a solution strategy.

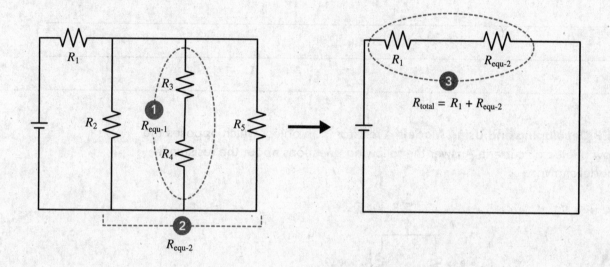

Step 1 The resistors in series can be added to find R_{equ-1}. Use the equation for resistors in series: $R_{equ-1} = R_3 + R_4$

Step 2 A second equivalent resistance (R_{equ-2}) can replace the resistors in parallel. Use the equation for resistors in parallel: $\frac{1}{R_{equ-2}} = \frac{1}{R_2} + \frac{1}{R_{equ-1}} + \frac{1}{R_5}$

Step 3 By drawing a new circuit diagram with R_{equ-2} replacing the parallel branches, it is easier to see that R_{equ-2} is in series with R_1. Use the equation for resistors in series to find R_{equ-3}, which is the total resistance:

$$R_{equ-3} = R_{total} = R_1 + R_{equ-2}$$

3-Dimensional Review

1. DCI Relationship Between Energy and Forces Describe how a uniform field will impact electron movement if two terminals of a battery are connected together using a silver wire.

_____

_____

_____

_____

_____

2. SEP Developing and Using Models A resistor is an object which opposes the flow of electric current. Answer the following questions about the resistance model shown:

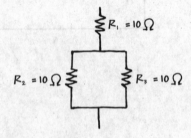

a. Are resistors 1 and 2 in series? Explain why or why not. _____

_____

b. What type of combination are resistors 2 and 3 in? What is their equivalent resistance? _____

c. Do resistors have equivalent greater resistance in parallel or in series? Explain why your answer makes sense based on the current.

_____

_____

_____

3. CCC Cause and Effect Current density is a vector quantity representing the amount of current flow through an area. Circle all of the following that would **not** result in an increased current.

a. increased drift velocity

b. decreased electric field

c. increased resistance

d. increased conductivity

Skills Practice

4. Three resistors are connected in a combination of series and parallel. Resistor R_1 is in series with the combination of resistors R_2 and R_3 in parallel. The resistors have resistance $R_1 = 8.000\ \Omega$, $R_2 = 8.000\ \Omega$, and $R_3 = 8.000\ \Omega$. Sketch a picture of the situation and determine the equivalent resistance of the combination of resistors.

5. Three resistors are connected in a combination of series and parallel. The combination of parallel resistors R_1 and R_2 is in series with resistor R_3. The resistors have resistance $R_1 = 12.00\ \Omega$, $R_2 = 13.00\ \Omega$, and $R_3 = 14.00\ \Omega$. Sketch a picture of the situation and determine the equivalent resistance of the combination of resistors.

6. Three resistors are connected in a combination of series and parallel. Resistor R_1 is in series with the combination of resistors R_2 and R_3 in parallel. The resistors have resistance $R_1 = 10.00\ \Omega$, $R_2 = 15.00\ \Omega$, and $R_3 = 20.00\ \Omega$. Determine the equivalent resistance of the combination of resistors.

a. $5.03\ \Omega$

b. $8.57\ \Omega$

c. $10.12\ \Omega$

d. $18.33\ \Omega$

Magnetic Forces and Fields

Magnetism is the result of moving charges. Atoms that have a greater number of unpaired electrons are likely to have a greater magnetic moment. Because they have magnetic properties, atoms can align magnetically into groups, or magnetic domains. Permanent magnets have permanently aligned magnetic domains, which results in two magnetic poles, called north and south, in the magnet. Attractive and repulsive forces caused by the magnetic field are strongest at these poles.

Current in a wire also generates a magnetic field perpendicular to the flow of current. The forces that magnetic fields exert are perpendicular to both the direction of the magnetic field and the direction of current flow. A moving charge within a magnetic field will experience a force. The magnitude of this force is described by the equation for the magnetic component of the Lorentz force.

Magnitude of the Magnetic Component of the Lorentz Force
$$F_M = qv_{perp}B$$
F_M = magnitude of the magnetic force q = charge v_{perp} = velocity perpendicular to the magnetic field B = magnetic field

The right hand rule (for positive charges) and the left hand rule (for negative charges) can be used to determine the direction of the force. In a uniform magnetic field, the magnetic component of the Lorentz force causes a moving charge to follow a circular path.

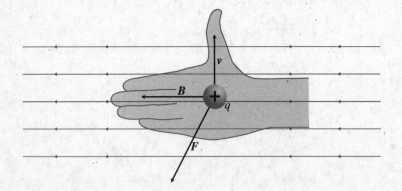 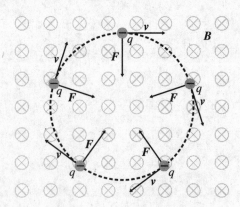

Use Models Use the left hand rule to explain the force direction shown for the electron at the top of the circle.

_____

_____

_____

_____

Mathematical Practices: Reason Abstractly and Quantitatively

Creating a coherent representation of a problem begins by attending to the meaning of quantities and their relationship with each other. When solving problems involving magnetic forces on moving charges, you will need to attend to the perpendicular relationship between the force, the magnetic field, and the velocity of the moving charge. In a vector diagram, one of these quantities will either point toward you or away from you. By convention, a circle with a dot represents a vector pointing toward you, as it looks like the pointed end of an arrow coming toward you. A circle with an x represents a vector pointing away from you, as it looks like the end of an arrow moving away from you. You can use the right hand rule or the left hand rule to show the direction of the magnetic force on the charged particle or object.

Use the right hand rule for a positive charge.

$B \odot \longrightarrow v_{perp}$

$\downarrow F_M$

magnetic field toward you

$F_M \uparrow$

$B \otimes \longrightarrow v_{perp}$

magnetic field away from you

$B \longleftarrow \odot v_{perp}$

$\downarrow F_M$

charge moving toward you

The magnetic force is directly proportional to the amount of charge, the perpendicular velocity of the charge, and the strength of the magnetic field ($F_M = qv_{perp}B$; q is assumed to be positive). Understanding this quantitative relationship is useful when reasoning about magnetic forces or checking a problem solution.

Sample Problem

A balloon gathers -1.0×10^{-6} C of charge as the wind blows it to the east through Earth's magnetic field at 1.8 m/s ($B_E = 5.0 \times 10^{-5}$ kg·C/s). Find the magnitude and direction of the magnetic force on the balloon.

1. Draw a Picture
The magnetic field of Earth points north and the charged balloon moves east.
The left hand rule must be used to determine the direction of the magnetic force because the balloon is negatively charged.
The force is directed down.

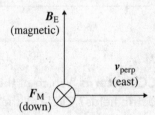

2. Apply Faraday's Law
$F_M = qv_{perp}B$
$F_M = (-1.0 \times 10^{-6} \text{ C})(1.8 \text{ m/s})(5.0 \times 10^{-5} \text{ kg·C/s}) = -9.0 \times 10^{-11} \text{ N}$

3. Check
The force has the correct units and mathematical sign. The force is small, which is consistent with the very weak forces due to Earth's magnetic field.

3-Dimensional Review

1. DCI Types of Interactions What causes magnetic force? How does that determine how two magnets interact?

_____

_____

_____

2. SEP Using Mathematics and Computational Thinking

    a. The Lorentz force equation is given by $F = qE + (qv \times B)$. Explain how this equation tells you what this force represents.

    _____

    _____

    b. The magnetic component of the Lorentz force uses a vector called the cross product. Why is this important?

    _____

    _____

    _____

    c. The magnetic force component of the Lorentz equation is $(qv \times B)$. In order to solve for the magnitude of the magnetic force, however, you can simply use $F_M = qv_{perp}B$. Based on these two equations, what is likely the purpose of the cross product in the Lorentz equation?

    _____

    _____

    _____

3. CCC Patterns Which of the following is a pattern shared by magnetic and electric fields? Circle all that apply.

    a. They are produced by charges.

    b. They have a north and south pole.

    c. The force gets stronger as distance decreases.

    d. Movement within is perpendicular to the field.

Skills Practice

4. You rub a small glass ball with a piece of silk, giving the ball a charge of 1.21×10^{-8} C. Determine the magnitude and direction of the force due to Earth's magnetic field ($B_E = 5.01 \times 10^{-5}$ T) if you throw the ball with a velocity of 9.41 m/s toward geographic East.

5. A particle with a charge of 11.2 μC moves with a velocity of 11.7 m/s toward geographic West ($B_E = 5.01 \times 10^{-5}$ T). If the Lorentz force on the particle is 9.12×10^{-9} N, what is the magnitude and direction of the electric field?

6. A balloon gathers −0.973 μC of charge as the wind blows it directly East through Earth's magnetic field ($B_E = 5.01 \times 10^{-5}$ T). If the magnetic force on the balloon is 8.11×10^{-10} N West, what is the velocity of the balloon?

a. −16.6 m/s

b. 3.95×10^{-20} m/s

c. 8.44 m/s

d. 16.6 m/s

Inducing Magnetism

Current generates a magnetic field, so a current-carrying wire will experience a force when it is placed within a magnetic field. The magnitude of the force (F) is equal to the product of the length of the wire (l), the current (I) running through the wire, and the strength of the magnetic field (B), or $F = IlB$.

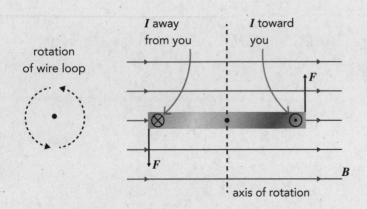

A current-carrying loop of wire in a magnetic field will experience torques that act in opposite directions on each side of the loop, which causes the loop to rotate. This is how motors use magnetism to make an axle rotate.

When a wire is shaped into a coil of several loops called a solenoid, there is a strong magnetic field through the center of the coil. The coiling movement of charged particles in Earth's core also generates a magnetic field with a north-south orientation that switches periodically over long periods of time.

Magnetic fields around wires, wire loops, and solenoids can be represented using field lines. The strength of each of these fields is represented by different versions of the Biot Savart law.

Biot Savart Laws for Current-Carrying Wires of Different Types

Straight Wire	Circular Loop	Solenoid
$B = \dfrac{\mu_0 I}{2\pi r}$	$B_{center} = \dfrac{\mu_0 I}{2R}$	$B_{inside} = \dfrac{\mu_0 NI}{l}$
r = distance from the wire	R = radius of loop	N = number of loops l = length of solenoid
B = magnitude of the magnetic field μ_0 = permeability of free space ($4\pi \times 10^{-7}$ T·m/A) I = current		

Identify Variables Does the strength of the magnetic field through a solenoid depend on the radius of the solenoid? Explain.

_____

_____

Mathematical Practices: Model with Mathematics

Equations model the mathematical relationships among quantities that scientists observe in real world phenomena. For this reason, they can be used to make predictions or draw conclusions.

Consider how the different versions of the Biot Savart law can be used to make predictions about the strength of the magnetic field around current-carrying wires, loops, or solenoids.

Scenario	Biot Savart equation	Prediction
An engineer is designing an electric motor. In order to increase the strength of the magnetic field through the wire loop, should the engineer increase or decrease the radius of the loop?	$B_{center} = \dfrac{\mu_0 I}{2R}$	Decreasing the radius (R) will increase the magnitude of the magnetic field through the center of the loop (B_{center}).
The magnetic domains of a ferromagnetic material can be aligned by placing the material within the strong magnetic field that runs through a current-carrying solenoid. Which solenoid will provide the strongest magnetic field, a 25 cm solenoid with 100 loops or a 75 cm solenoid with 200 loops?	$B_{inside} = \dfrac{\mu_0 NI}{l}$	The magnitude of the magnetic field (B_{inside}) is proportional to $\dfrac{N}{l}$. The 25 cm solenoid with 100 loops will provide a stronger magnetic field because: $$\dfrac{100}{25} > \dfrac{200}{75}$$
Earth's magnetic dynamo depends on the helical movement of charged particles in Earth's core. What changes in the motion of the particles could reduce the strength of Earth's magnetic field? How could a cooling core cause these changes?	$B_{inside} = \dfrac{\mu_0 NI}{l}$	The field will weaken if the number of charged particles traveling through the core decreases (I decreases). As the core cools, fewer charged particles will have enough energy to move through the dense core.

3-Dimensional Review

1. DCI Types of Interactions What happens to a current-carrying wire when it is placed within a magnetic field? Explain your answer.

_____

_____

_____

2. SEP Using Mathematics and Computational Thinking

a. The magnitude of the magnetic field for a straight, current-carrying wire can be found by $B = \left(\frac{\mu_0 I}{2\pi r}\right)$. If the distance from the wire was cut by a third, what would happen to the magnitude of the magnetic field?

_____

_____

b. At a time, 0, the magnetic field at the center of a current-carrying loop is $B = \frac{\mu_0 I}{2R}$. If the current is cut in half and the magnitude of the magnetic field doubled, what happens to the radius of the loop?

_____

_____

c. The magnetic field in a solenoid is given by $B_{\text{inside}} = \frac{\mu_0 NI}{l}$. If you want to double the number of loops without changing the magnitude of the magnetic field, what two things could you do?

_____

_____

3. CCC Patterns Which of the following is a pattern for the magnetic field inside current-carrying straight, loop, and solenoid wires? Circle all that apply.

a. The magnitude of the magnetic field is directly proportional to the number of loops.

b. The magnitude of the magnetic field is directly proportional to the current.

c. The magnitude of the magnetic field is inversely proportional to the radius of the wire.

d. The magnitude of the magnetic field is dependent on the permeability of free space.

Skills Practice

4. A straight wire carries a current of 14.1 A. What percent greater is the magnitude of the magnetic field at a distance of 1.82 m than at a distance of 11.8 meters?

5. A solenoid with 3600 loops carries a 16.00-A current. If for a particular electromagnet the solenoid should have a magnetic field of 0.4700 T, what is the length of the solenoid?

6. A wire loop with a radius of 0.16 m carries a current of 19.8 A. Which of the following will double the magnetic field at the center of the loop? Circle all that apply.

a. decreasing the radius of the loop by 50%

b. decreasing the radius of the loop by 75% while increasing the current by 50%

c. halving the radius of the loop while doubling the current

d. doubling the radius of the loop while quadrupling the current

Inducing Current

When the magnetic field through an area (called magnetic flux) changes, it can induce current in a conductive material, such as a loop or coil of wire. Magnetic flux (Φ) equals the product of the area (A) and the magnetic field perpendicular to the area (B_{perp}), or $\Phi = B_{perp}A$. Magnetic flux can be changed by moving a magnet through a loop or coil or by changing the area of a wire loop or coil that is near a magnet, either by rotating the loop or changing its size.

Changing the magnetic flux through a loop or coil of wire induces an electromotive force (EMF) that accelerates electrons in the wire. EMF is the measure of the electrical action produced when magnetic energy (or another energy type) is converted into electrical energy. EMF is measured in volts. Faraday's law describes how induced EMF (V_ε) depends on the number of loops (N) in the wire coil and the rate of change of magnetic flux $\left(\frac{\Delta\Phi}{\Delta t}\right)$. According to Lenz's law, the induced current and induced magnetic field oppose the change in flux. In the diagram, the change in flux is down, so the induced magnetic field is directed up.

Faraday's Law
$$V_\varepsilon = -N\frac{\Delta\Phi}{\Delta t}$$
V_ε = induced electromotive force $\frac{\Delta\Phi}{\Delta t}$ = rate of change of
N = number of wire coils   magnetic flux

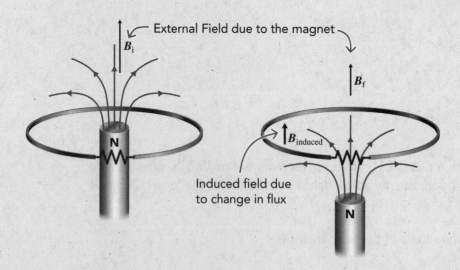

External Field due to the magnet

B_i

B_f

$B_{induced}$

Induced field due to change in flux

N

N

Reason Quantitatively According to Faraday's law, how can you change the system in the diagram to increase the induced EMF?

_____

_____

Mathematical Practices: Make Sense of Problems

Motional EMF is generated when a magnetic field surrounds a conductive bar moving along two metal rails that are connected by a current-carrying wire. The induced EMF changes as the area of the rectangular loop formed by the system increases or decreases. Drawing a diagram can help you make sense of motional EMF problems.

Establish a direction for the magnetic field surrounding the system. The induced magnetic field will be in the opposite direction.

The change in flux is due to the rate of change in area $\left(\frac{l\Delta x}{\Delta t}\right)$. Use a velocity vector to show which way the metal bar moves.

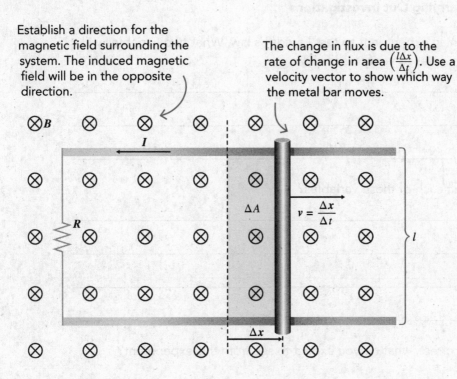

Once you have determined the direction of the induced magnetic field, you can use the right hand rule to find the current direction. In this example, the induced field points out of the page, so the current travels counterclockwise through the loop.

Being aware of the different ways that the change in flux may be represented in the equation for Faraday's law will be helpful as you develop a solution strategy for motional EMF problems. You can select the version of the equation that aligns best to the known and unknown quantities in the problem.

Versions of Faraday's Law

$$V_\varepsilon = -N\frac{\Delta\Phi}{\Delta t} = \frac{(B\Delta A)}{\Delta t} = Bl\left(\frac{\Delta x}{\Delta t}\right) = Blv$$

V_ε = induced electromotive force

N = number of loops

$\frac{\Delta\Phi}{\Delta t}$ = rate of change of magnetic flux

B = magnitude of the induced magnetic field

ΔA = change in area of the loop

l = distance between rails

$\frac{\Delta x}{\Delta t} = v$ = velocity of the metal bar

3-Dimensional Review

1. DCI Types of Interactions Describe, in your own words, the interaction between magnetic flux, EMF, and induced current and magnetic field.

_____

_____

2. SEP Planning and Carrying Out Investigations

   a. You want to design an experiment to test Faraday's law. What two variables will you need to test in order to verify his law?

     _____

     _____

     _____

   b. How might you test each of these variables?

     _____

     _____

     _____

     _____

   c. If Faraday's law is correct, what do you expect to see from this experiment?

     _____

     _____

3. CCC Cause and Effect According to Faraday's law, which of the following will produce a current in a wire loop? Circle all that apply.

   a. holding a magnet at a set distance from the wire loop

   b. increasing the area of the wire loop

   c. moving a magnet away from the wire loop

   d. holding a magnet at a set distance from two wire loops with different areas

Skills Practice

4. A square loop with sides of length 1.1 m is oriented parallel to the y and z axes. A uniform magnetic field passes through the loop. The field is $B = (1.4\text{ T})\hat{x} + (0.8\text{ T})\hat{y}$. Determine the magnetic flux through the loop.

5. Two rails separated by a distance of 1.03 m are connected by a fixed wire on the left end and a movable metal rod on the right, forming a loop. A uniform magnetic field with magnitude 2.24 T points toward you through the loop. You move the rod to the left with a speed of 5.33 m/s. Calculate the induced EMF and determine the direction of the current.

6. Two rails are connected by a fixed wire on the left and a moveable metal rod on the right forming a loop. Which of the following scenarios will produce an induced EMF in the clockwise direction? Circle all that apply.

   a. A uniform magnetic field points **toward you** through the loop. You move the rod to the **left**.

   b. A uniform magnetic field points **toward you** through the loop. You move the rod to the **right**.

   c. A uniform magnetic field points **away from you** through the loop. You move the rod to the **left**.

   d. A uniform magnetic field points **away from you** through the loop. You move the rod to the **right**.

Atoms and Atomic Structure

Scientists determined the composition of the atom through observation and experimentation. They found that the atom includes negatively charged electrons orbiting a small positively charged nucleus. Once this was understood, patterns observed in the physical and chemical properties of the elements could be explained using Coulomb forces. The arrows in the diagram show trends in the characteristics of the elements.

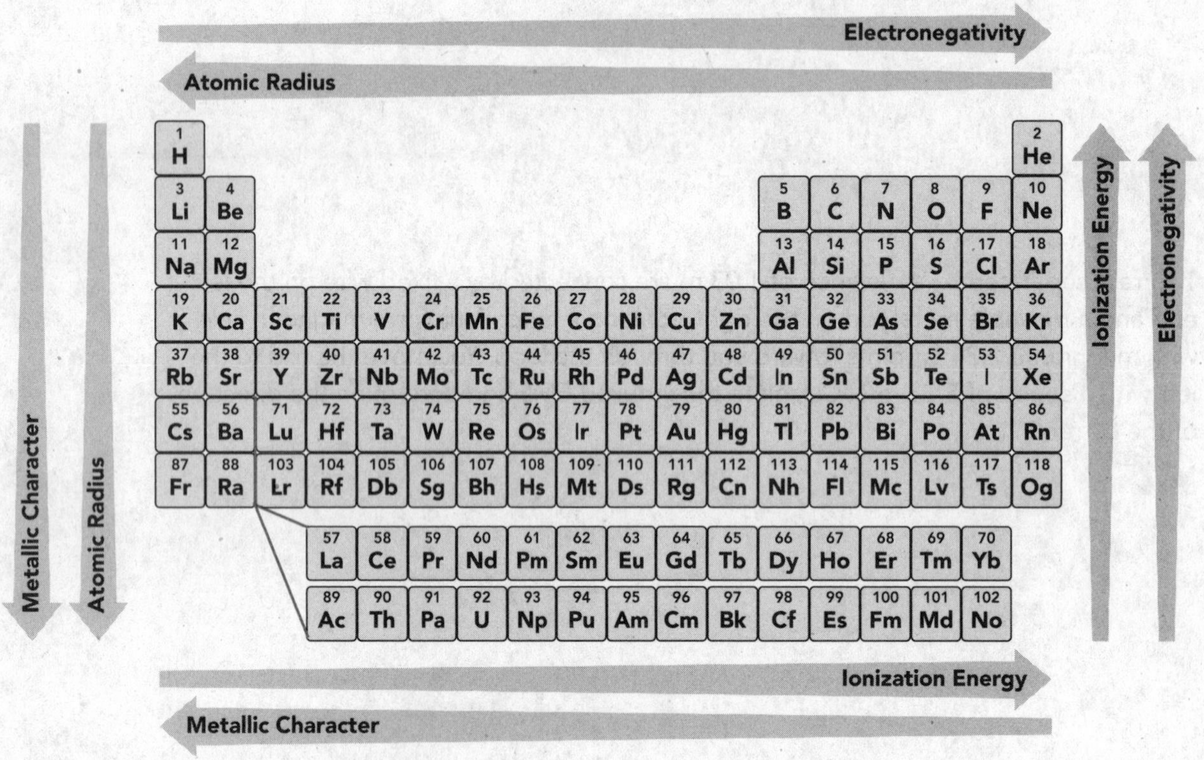

Across a period (row) of the table, the nucleus grows in mass and positive charge, pulling the electrons closer to the nucleus and increasing the energy needed to remove them from the atom. The atomic radius decreases and ionization energy increases. Electronegativity increases as the nucleus grows because the nucleus exerts a stronger pull on electrons shared in a chemical bond.

Down a group (column) of the table, inner electrons shield the valence electrons from the attractive force of the nucleus, so ionization energy and electronegativity decrease. The atomic radius expands to accommodate more "shells" of electrons.

Explain Phenomena Which element will have the higher ionization energy: lithium (Li) or potassium (K)? Why?

_____

_____

Science Practices: Use Mathematics

Scientists use mathematics to analyze data. They also use mathematics to support scientific claims. Equations reveal proportional relationships, which in turn, connect to cause-and-effect relationships observed in real world phenomena.

Magnetic Force and Electrons in Atoms

J.J. Thomson used a device similar to the one shown in the diagram when he discovered the electron. The tube is evacuated (empty), so the cathode ray must be composed of atoms or particles within atoms that are ejected from one electrode toward the other. Magnetic deflection of the ray reveals that the particles are negatively charged.

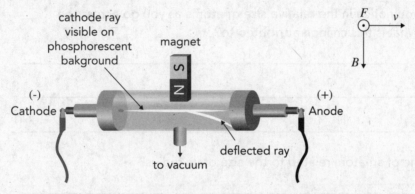

Scientists can use the equation for the magnitude of the magnetic force, $F_M = qvB$, to support this explanation. Recall that: F_M = magnetic force, q = charge, v = velocity perpendicular to the magnetic field, and B = magnitude of the magnetic field. If $q = 0$, then $F_M = 0$. Since there is a force on the ray, then $q \neq 0$. A charge must be present.

Coulomb's Law and Electronegativity

Scientists can use Coulomb's law to explain periodic trends in the electronegativity of elements. Coulomb's law states that the electric force (F_E) between two charged objects is directly proportional to the amount of charge on each object (q_1 and q_2) and inversely proportional to the square of the distance (r) between them (note: k is Coulomb's constant).

As the number of protons increases in elements listed from left to right on the table, q_1 increases while r^2 remains fairly constant, so F_E increases. The force on electrons shared in a bond will increase and electronegativity increases.

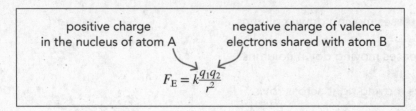

positive charge in the nucleus of atom A   negative charge of valence electrons shared with atom B

$$F_E = k\frac{q_1 q_2}{r^2}$$

Down a group of the periodic table, q_1 increases but r^2 increases faster. As r^2 increases, F_E decreases. The force on valence electrons shared in a bond will decrease and electronegativity decreases.

3-Dimensional Review

1. DCI Types of Interactions How did later models of the atom adjust for problems with the Rutherford model?

_____

_____

_____

_____

2. SEP Using Mathematics and Computational Thinking

a. What is a trend you notice in the relative size of atoms as you go across the periodic table? What is this change attributed to?

_____

_____

_____

b. How is the volume of an atom related to the size of its radius?

_____

_____

_____

c. Based on the equation for volume found above, rank copper, helium, lead, and silver from smallest to largest volume. Explain your answer.

_____

_____

_____

3. CCC Patterns Which of the following is a pattern on the Periodic Table? Circle all that apply.

a. metallic character decreases moving down columns

b. electronegativity decreases moving down columns

c. atomic radius increases moving right across rows

d. ionization energy increases moving right across rows

Skills Practice

4. A cathode ray is subjected to a magnetic field of strength 3.60 milliTeslas, which is directed perpendicular to the path of the ray. This interaction causes the path of the ray to bend in an arc of radius 19.9 cm. Use mathematics to write an equation to determine the speed of each electron in the beam, then solve.

5. Two point charges have charges of $q_1 = 8.7\ \mu C$ and $q_2 = -9.1\ \mu C$. The magnitude of the net electric force on q_1 is 42 N. Use mathematics to write an equation to determine the distance between q_1 and q_2, then solve.

6. A cathode ray is subjected to a magnetic field of unknown strength, which is directed perpendicular to the path of the ray. This interaction causes the path of the ray to bend in an arc. Use mathematics to determine which equation will accurately solve for the magnetic field strength.

a. $B = \frac{mv^2}{Rq}$

b. $B = \frac{mv}{Rq}$

c. $B = \frac{Rqv}{m}$

d. $B = \frac{Rq}{mv^2}$

Attractive and Repulsive Forces

Coulomb forces hold ions together in ionic bonds. They also determine whether valence electrons held in covalent bonds will be shared equally or unequally between two atoms. Metallic bonds are similar to covalent bonds in that valence electrons interact with multiple nuclei, but each electron is able to move relatively freely among all of the nuclei within a metal lattice.

Molecules can also experience Coulomb forces, which scientists refer to as intermolecular interactions or intermolecular forces. The strength of the intermolecular forces between particles in a material defines the state of the material at a given temperature. As temperature increases, atoms and molecules gain energy that allows them to escape the intermolecular forces holding them together.

States of Matter Whether a material is a solid, liquid, or gas is explained by the strength of the forces between the particles and the energy of the particles.

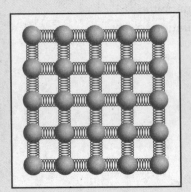 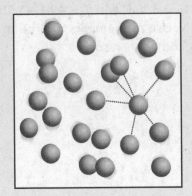 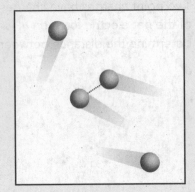

Intermolecular forces also explain why different substances are in different states at the same temperature. For example, hydrogen molecules only experience weak van der Waals interactions so the boiling point of hydrogen is low and it is a gas at room temperature. In contrast, water molecules form hydrogen bonds, which are much stronger than van der Waals interactions. As a result, the boiling point of water is high and it is a liquid at room temperature.

Use Models How are the intermolecular interactions represented differently in the solid model and the gas model and why?

_____

_____

_____

_____

Science Practices: Construct Explanations

Using clear cause-and-effect statements is important when constructing explanations. Sometimes a series of cause-and-effect statements are needed to explain a phenomenon completely. Effective explanations also rely on correct scientific understandings.

How would you explain what causes crystalline substances to break along flat planes while many other substances crumble or break along jagged edges? The diagrams provide clues about the cause-and-effect relationships needed to construct a complete explanation.

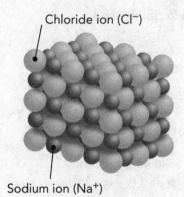

Chloride ion (Cl⁻)

Sodium ion (Na⁺)

Cause: Chloride ions and sodium ions form an ionic lattice.

Effect: The lattice is strong because the cations (Na⁺) and anions (Cl⁻) attract each other on all sides.

Understanding: The electronegativity difference between the two atoms is large. The atoms ionize and Coulomb forces pull the ions together.

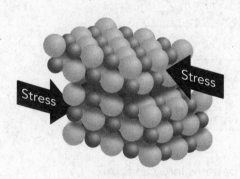

Stress

Stress

Cause: Stress forces are applied parallel to the planes of connection in the ionic lattice.

Effect: The ions slide past each other so that same-charge ions are closer together.

Understanding: The stress forces must be strong enough to overcome the Coulomb forces between the ions.

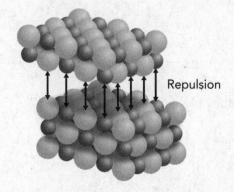

Repulsion

Cause: Same-charge ions repel each other at multiple locations.

Effect: The lattice breaks along a flat plane instead of crumbling or breaking along a jagged edge.

Understanding: The pattern of alternating ions makes fracture more likely. Substances that lack this pattern, like metal lattices, do not fracture in this way. Metals deform under stress instead.

3-Dimensional Review

1. DCI Types of Interactions What is the difference between a covalent bond and a metallic bond?

_____

_____

_____

_____

2. SEP Using Mathematics and Computational Thinking

   a. In your own words, explain why ionic solids have higher melting points than covalent solids or metallic solids.

     _____

     _____

     _____

   b. Circle the appropriate mathematical symbol to complete the following sentence. The energy of a liquid is typically (>, <, =) the energy of a solid, and (>, <, =) the energy of a gas.

   c. Explain how your answer for part B is true.

     _____

     _____

     _____

3. CCC Patterns Which of the following is true of the lattice patterns ions can form? Circle all that apply.

   a. Ions in crystals line up in repeating geometric shapes.

   b. Each cation attracts other cations on all sides.

   c. Each anion attracts cations on all sides.

   d. The pattern responds well to bending and sliding, so they break less easily than metals.

Skills Practice

4. Use an understanding of forces between particles to construct an explanation for how ionic bonds form. How does this form lattice patterns?

_____

_____

_____

_____

_____

_____

_____

5. Construct an explanation for how hydrogen and oxygen in an H_2O molecule bond using electric forces. What type of bond is this?

_____

_____

_____

_____

_____

_____

_____

6. Which bond is explained by the following scenario? In this bond, valence electrons cease to be bound to one nucleus and instead interact with multiple nuclei. Each electron is able to move relatively freely among all of the nuclei in the sample.

a. ionic bond

b. covalent bond

c. metallic bond

d. none of the above

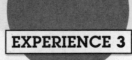
Material Properties

The properties of materials are determined by interactions at the atomic and molecular level. For example, substances have low electrical conductivity when valence electrons within the material are bound tightly to one or more atomic nuclei. Metals are generally excellent conductors of electricity because valence electrons can travel between atomic nuclei in the metal lattice.

Solids vary in the arrangement and attraction between internal particles, so they also vary in their rigidity. This means that they deform by different amounts when they experience stress. Mechanical stress can be described by its direction (shear or normal) and by its cause. If an object deforms under stress, the strain the object experiences is determined by the fractional change in the object's length in each dimension. A pliable material has a low Young's modulus, which is the ratio of stress to strain. If stress is applied in three dimensions, the bulk modulus can be used to measure a substance's resistance to compression.

Stress	Strain	Young's Modulus	Bulk Modulus
$\sigma = \dfrac{F}{A}$	$\varepsilon = \dfrac{\Delta L}{L}$	$E = \dfrac{\text{stress}}{\text{strain}} = \dfrac{\frac{F}{A}}{\frac{\Delta L}{L}} = \dfrac{F \cdot L}{\Delta L \cdot A}$	$B = \dfrac{-V \Delta P}{\Delta V}$

σ = stress	F = force	A = resisting area
ε = strain	ΔL = change in length	L = original length
E = Young's modulus	B = bulk modulus	V = original volume
ΔP = change in pressure	ΔV = change in volume	

Warped Shelves

The effect of pressure, or stress, on the top and bottom of this shelf is different.

Synthesize Information Does the shelf experience strain along its top surface or its bottom surface?

_____

_____

Based on evidence in the drawing, does the shelf have a high or low Young's modulus? Explain.

_____

_____

Mathematical Practices: Make Sense of Problems

You will need to evaluate key differences between stress and strain, and between Young's modulus and bulk modulus when making sense of problems involving mechanical stress. Force is perpendicular (normal) to the resisting area for stress due to compression or tension, while force is parallel to the resisting area for shear stress. Drawing a picture will help you make sense of force directions. Young's modulus applies to solids experiencing an external force applied in a single direction. Bulk modulus applies to solids or liquids experiencing external forces from all directions.

Sample Problem

Engineers test composite posts for their ability to withstand shear stress from heavy, sliding objects. To match the force the posts will experience, they apply a 5000 N force at a 45° angle to the top of the post, which has a radius of 0.25 m. The engineers need the post to have a Young's modulus of 20 MPa or higher. During the test, the post's length increases from 2.500 m to 2.502 m.

a) What shear stress does the post experience?

b) Does the composite material meet the Young's modulus minimum?

Draw a Picture

Drawing a picture will help you make sense of the force applied to the post. The 50,000 N force is at a 45° angle. Only the parallel component of force will contribute to shear stress.

$$5000 \text{ N } (\sin 45°) = F_{\text{parallel}} = 3536 \text{ N}$$

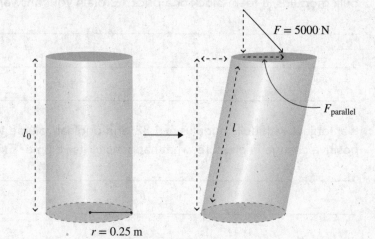

Solve

a. To find the shear stress:

The shear stress depends on the resisting area. The picture will also help you observe that the resisting area is the area of a circle, or πr^2.

$$\sigma = \frac{F}{A} = \frac{F_{\text{parallel}}}{\pi r^2} = \frac{3536 \text{ N}}{\pi (0.25 \text{ m})^2} = 18,040 \text{ Pa}$$

b. To find and compare the Young's modulus:

$$Y = \frac{\text{stress}}{\text{strain}} = \frac{18,040 \text{ Pa}}{\left(\frac{\Delta l}{l_0}\right)} = \frac{18,040 \text{ Pa}}{\left(\frac{0.002 \text{ m}}{2.50 \text{ m}}\right)} = 22,550,000 \text{ Pa or 23 MPa}$$

Yes, the composite material meets the Young's modulus minimum.

3-Dimensional Review

1. DCI Types of Interactions Explain in your own words how the strength of the collective intermolecular forces within an object impact its stress and strain.

_____

_____

_____

_____

2. SEP Using Mathematics and Computational Thinking

a. The bulk modulus of an object can be found by $B = \frac{-V\Delta P}{\Delta V}$. Using the equation, describe what the bulk modulus is in your own words.

_____

_____

_____

b. Based on your previous answer, which of the following is likely to have a larger bulk modulus, a foam block or a brick? Explain your answer.

_____

_____

_____

c. If an object with bulk modulus of 1.82, and original volume V, undergoes a positive change in pressure, what happens to its volume? Explain your answer.

_____

_____

_____

3. CCC Patterns Which of the following is a pattern with stress and strain? Circle all that apply.

a. Strain is inversely proportional to stress.

b. Strain is inversely proportional to length.

c. Stress is directly proportional to strain.

d. Stress is directly proportional to the cross-sectional area.

Skills Practice

4. The bulk modulus of sapphire is 2.40×10^{11} Pa. Determine the change in volume (in cm^3) experienced by a sapphire that is taken from an environment of 96,227 Pa pressure to an environment at 118,945 Pa. The original volume of the sapphire is 0.0730 cm^3.

5. Students in an art class are pouring a homogeneous mixture of 54.0% silver and 46.0% nickel for use in casting small statues. Given the known density of pure solid silver (10.5 g/cm^3) and of pure solid nickel (8.91 g/cm^3), determine the density of the alloy that is created.

6. The bulk modulus of stone is 3.81×10^{11} Pa. Determine the original volume (in cm^3) experienced by the stone when it is taken from an environment of 96,227 Pa pressure to an environment at 118,945 Pa. The change in volume of the stone is -5.72×10^{-9} cm^3.

a. 3.41×10^{-16} cm^3

b. 0.0959 cm^3

c. 3.44 cm^3

d. 1.51×10^{24} cm^3

Structure and Function

Polymers are chains made up of smaller molecules called monomers. Natural polymers include polysaccharide carbohydrates, proteins, and nucleic acids such as DNA and RNA. Synthetic polymers include nylon, neoprene, and plastics. Elastomers, like rubber, are natural or synthetic polymers that are highly elastic at ambient temperatures. The structure of polymers gives them a variety of useful properties. For example, bakers observe the stretchy properties of the wheat proteins gliadin and glutenin when shaping pizza dough into a broad, thin disk.

In general, polymers are flexible and strong. They can fold to form a variety of complex shapes or twist together to make very strong fibers. Scientists and engineers use an understanding of the structure and function of polymers to design solutions to various problems. For example, biomedical engineers take advantage of the folding properties of protein polymers to make synthetic hormones that mimic the action of natural hormones in the body. The model shows how a hormone fits into a receptor like a key fits into a lock in order to initiate a change in a cell. An engineered (or synthetic) protein can do the same job if it fits the receptor in the same way and if it has the same chemical properties.

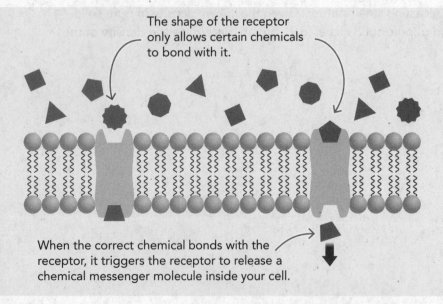

The shape of the receptor only allows certain chemicals to bond with it.

When the correct chemical bonds with the receptor, it triggers the receptor to release a chemical messenger molecule inside your cell.

Apply Scientific Reasoning The DNA polymer is made up of four different nucleotide monomers: adenine (A), guanine (G), cytosine (C), and thymine (T). A strand of DNA will have these monomers in a specific order, such as GACTTACT. Use this information and the analogy of letters in words to explain how the polymer structure of DNA allows it to store information.

_____

_____

_____

Science Practices: Designing Solutions

Engineers make use of the structure and function of polymers as they design solutions to meet human needs and wants. Because polymers are chains of monomers, they can have chemical groups spaced at regular intervals that allow for cross-linking. As a result, polymer strands can connect together into sheets or twisted fibers. The microtubules that support cell structure, vulcanized rubber in shoe soles, and polyethylene in plastic bags are examples of materials made from linked polymers. The diagram shows how polymer strands come together in nylon, a stretchy synthetic fiber.

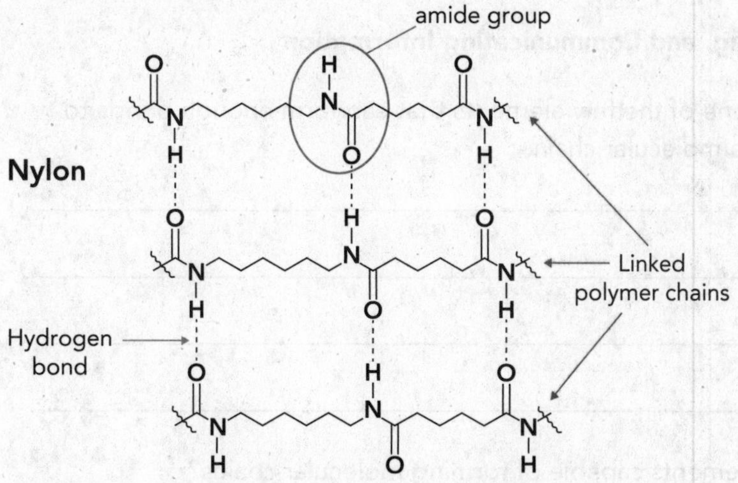

Nylon is a general name for a family of elastomers with a range of properties. Each type is made from monomers with amide groups that can crosslink with each other through hydrogen bonding. Nylon is used in textiles, containers for boil-in-the bag foods, rope, and many other applications. Engineers identified these uses for nylon polymers because of their physical properties. Consider how the structure and function of nylon makes it useful for athletic clothing:

- **Elasticity:** Athletic clothing needs to be flexible. The Young's modulus of some nylon materials is very low, meaning that they deform easily without tearing when stressed. As the diagram shows, there are long hydrocarbon regions of the polymers which experience only very weak Coulomb forces, punctuated by amide groups (circled in the diagram) that form strong hydrogen bonds. This structure allows the polymers to slide along one another without separating.

- **Heat resistance:** Like the hydrogen bonds between water molecules, the hydrogen bonds that hold nylon polymers together allow nylon to resist changes in temperature. It stays cool while absorbing heat from a person's body.

- **Water absorption:** The amide groups along the nylon polymer attract water. Nylon absorbs moisture, wicking sweat away from an athlete's skin.

3-Dimensional Review

1. DCI Types of Interactions How do polymers form? What are the benefits of natural and synthetic polymers?

_____

_____

_____

_____

2. SEP Obtaining, Evaluating, and Communicating Information

a. Explain why carbon is one of the few elements that can form enough bonds to be the "backbone" of a molecular chain.

_____

_____

_____

_____

b. Why are only certain elements capable of forming molecular chains?

_____

_____

_____

c. What differentiates an elastomer from other polymers?

_____

_____

_____

3. CCC Structure and Function A scientist is designing a new material to cover their cold-weather instruments. Which of the following would they consider?

a. natural rubber

b. glutenin

c. neoprene

d. protein

Skills Practice

4. A patient is at the doctor for a slow heart rate due to low levels of adrenaline. The doctor recommends an agonist to the patient to increase their heart rate. In your own words, explain how an agonist functions in order to increase the heart rate of the patient.

_____

_____

_____

_____

_____

_____

5. A patient sees a doctor for high blood pressure. If adrenaline is dangerous for patients with high blood pressure, why might a doctor recommend a beta blocker whose structure mimics adrenaline?

_____

_____

_____

_____

_____

_____

6. The previous two problems use examples of "lock-and-key" receptors. If a doctor is looking for a key-like receptor that will **not** activate a receptor molecule, which of the following are they looking for?

a. antagonist

b. agonist

c. protein receptor

d. chemical messenger molecule

Classifying Work and Energy

Work can either be done on a system (positive work) or by a system (negative work). Determining the work done requires defining the system and comparing the direction of the net external force and the displacement of the system. When positive work is done on a system, the system's kinetic energy changes.

Work	Work-Energy Theorem
$W = Fd\cos\theta$	$W_{total} = \Delta KE = KE_f - KE_i$
W = work	W_{total} = total work done on a system
F = force	ΔKE = change in kinetic energy of a system
d = displacement	KE_i = initial kinetic energy
θ = angle between force and displacement	KE_f = final kinetic energy

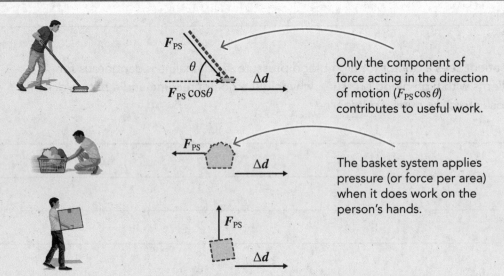

Only the component of force acting in the direction of motion ($F_{PS}\cos\theta$) contributes to useful work.

The basket system applies pressure (or force per area) when it does work on the person's hands.

When work is done on a system, energy external to the system must be supplied, and the transfer of energy can happen at different rates. Power is the rate at which work is done or energy is transmitted over time.

Power
$P = \dfrac{W}{\Delta t}$
P = power W = work Δt = change in time

Apply Mathematical Concepts Suppose the person carrying the box lets it go and it falls to the ground. Is work being done on the box when it falls? Explain.

_____

_____

What are three ways to increase the power of a broom stroke?

_____

Mathematical Practices: Model with Mathematics

An energy bar chart is a useful tool for visualizing the effect of work on a real-world system. The energy bar chart below shows the effect of braking force on a moving car. The force direction and displacement direction are opposite because friction (f_k) from the road slows the car down as the brakes slow the forward rotation of the car's tires.

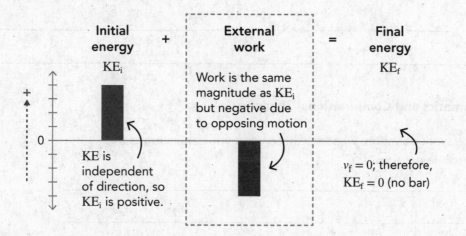

Once an energy bar chart is complete, you can translate it into a mathematical equation using the work-energy theorem.

$$KE_i + W = KE_f \rightarrow \tfrac{1}{2}mv_i^2 + f_k d\cos\theta = \tfrac{1}{2}mv_f^2$$

Notice that the bar chart can help you assign correct mathematical signs to quantities as you enter them into the equation. For example, because the work done by the brakes is in the opposite direction of the car's motion, you can establish the sign convention shown. If you assign a positive value to d, the displacement of the car as it slows down, it determines that the value of f_k will be negative.

Energy bar charts can represent more complex systems, such as when more than one external force is acting on an object or when work on an object converts an object's potential energy to kinetic energy.

To construct an energy bar chart:

1. Define the system and identify the forms of energy present in the initial and final states.

2. Analyze the forces that act on the system to identify what external work is done and in what direction.

3. Draw a bar for each form of energy present in the initial and final states, and for work done on the system. The length of each bar should be equivalent to the amount of energy present.

4. Use the energy bar chart to write a mathematical equation.

3-Dimensional Review

1. DCI Definitions of Energy In your own words, give new examples of positive work, negative work, and no work being done.

_____

_____

_____

_____

2. SEP Using Mathematics and Computational Thinking

a. According to the work equation, what are three ways you can increase the amount of work done on a system?

_____

_____

b. According to the Work-Energy Theorem, increasing the final kinetic energy will only increase the work done in what conditions?

_____

_____

_____

c. According to the power equation, if the amount of work stays the same, will increasing the amount of time increase or decrease power? Explain your answer.

_____

_____

_____

3. CCC Systems and System Models Which scenario will have the greatest amount of total work done by the system?

a. a roller coaster going from 20 m/s to 35 m/s

b. a roller coaster going from 35 m/s to 20 m/s

c. a roller coaster going from 40 m/s to 50 m/s

d. a roller coaster going from 50 m/s to 40 m/s

Skills Practice

4. A 1.04-kg binder is initially at rest on a wood desk. The binder is then pushed with a constant force of 4.2 N. Friction with a magnitude of 1.8 N is exerted on the moving binder by the surface of the desk. Draw an energy bar chart of the situation. Then determine the final velocity of the binder after it has been pushed 0.70 meters across the table.

5. A 0.05-kg foosball is initially at rest on a table. The foosball is then pushed with a constant force of 8.3 N. Friction with a magnitude of 0.5 N is exerted on the moving ball by the surface of the table. Draw an energy bar chart of the situation. Then determine the final velocity of the ball after it has been pushed 0.20 meters across the table.

6. A 2.08-kg dinner platter is initially at rest on a dining table. The platter is then pushed in the positive direction with a constant force of 2.6 N. Friction with a magnitude of 1.04 N is exerted on the moving platter by the surface of the table. Determine the final velocity of the platter after it has been pushed 0.30 meters across the table.

    a. −3.3 m/s

    b. −0.7 m/s

    c. 0.7 m/s

    d. 3.3 m/s

Mechanical Energy

A system can have potential energy due to the relative position of its objects. There are different types of potential energy, including gravitational, elastic, electrostatic, intermolecular, nuclear, chemical, and magnetic potential energy. Potential energy can be thought of as stored energy that has the ability to do work.

An object that stores energy because it is above the ground in Earth's gravitational field can do work when it falls. Similarly, the energy stored in a compressed spring can do work when the spring is released.

Elastic Potential Energy	Gravitational Potential Energy
$$PE_s = \frac{1}{2} k_s x^2$$ PE_s = elastic potential energy k_s = spring constant x = displacement of spring from rest	$$\Delta PE_g = mg(\Delta h)$$ ΔPE_g = change in gravitational potential energy m = mass g = acceleration due to gravity = 9.8 m/s^2 Δh = change in height

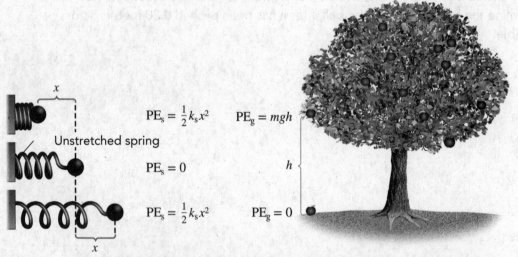

$$PE_s = \frac{1}{2} k_s x^2 \qquad PE_g = mgh$$

Unstretched spring

$$PE_s = 0$$

$$PE_s = \frac{1}{2} k_s x^2 \qquad PE_g = 0$$

A recoiling spring and a falling apple are examples of mechanical systems in which potential energy transforms into kinetic energy. The mechanical energy of a system refers to the sum of potential energies and kinetic energies in the system. To change the mechanical energy of a system, work must be done on the system. For example, friction changes the mechanical energy of a system by converting kinetic energy into heat.

Construct an Explanation Briefly explain how a person does work on a spring to change its potential energy.

_____

_____

_____

Mathematical Practices: Reason Abstractly and Quantitatively

Several different quantities and their mathematical relationships may need consideration when solving problems involving mechanical systems. Drawing a picture of the scenario will be helpful when defining the system and identifying known and unknown quantities. Constructing an energy bar chart that includes both potential and kinetic energies will be helpful in writing mathematical equations that describe the relationships among quantities.

This drawing helps you identify:

- the system
- where the rollercoaster has potential energy, kinetic energy, or both
- quantities that you will need to calculate energies and work (e.g. v_i, v_f, f_k)
- external forces that do work on the system

External Work
A rollercoaster car rushes downhill and then comes to a complete stop after the brakes are applied.

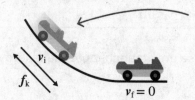

PE is converted into KE as the car travels down the hill.

This energy bar chart helps you visualize the initial and final energies of the system and how external work affects the system.

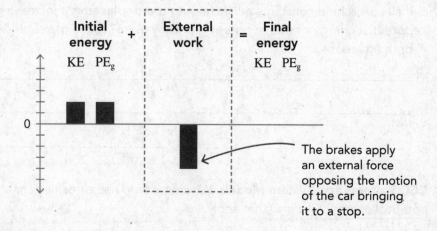

The brakes apply an external force opposing the motion of the car bringing it to a stop.

The energy bar chart also helps you construct a mathematical equation to represent the system. Each bar in the chart is associated with a different equation. The initial energies and external work sum to give the final energy of the roller coaster system. Because the rollercoaster car is at rest at the bottom of the hill, the final energy of the system equals zero.

$$\left(\tfrac{1}{2}mv_i^2 + mgh_i\right) + W_{\text{brakes}} = 0$$

3-Dimensional Review

1. DCI Definitions of Energy In your own words, describe gravitational potential energy and elastic potential energy. How do you increase each type of energy?

_____

_____

_____

_____

2. SEP Using Mathematics and Computational Thinking

a. How are the gravitational potential energy and elastic potential energy equations related?

_____

b. How do you decrease gravitational potential energy? What about elastic potential energy?

_____

_____

_____

c. If all else is held constant, will increasing the displacement increase gravitational potential energy or elastic potential energy more? Explain your answer based on both equations.

_____

_____

_____

3. CCC Systems and System Models Which scenario has a positive change in potential energy? Circle all that apply.

a. a frisbee tossed from arm level that gets caught in a tree

b. a rubber band around some pens that stretches to fit 5 more pens

c. a spring that recoils after just being released

d. a pencil sitting on a desk that falls to the ground

Skills Practice

4. A friend stands in a treehouse 4.95 m off the ground. She drops a bowling ball of mass 4.98 kg onto a highly elastic trampoline 1.02 m above the ground. The bowling ball lands on the trampoline, which stretches downward until the ball stops, just barely before touching the ground. Sketch an energy bar chart of the situation. What is the elastic spring constant of the trampoline fabric?

5. A friend stands in a treehouse 6.00 m off the ground. He drops a bowling ball of mass 3.81 kg onto a highly elastic trampoline 20.9 cm above the ground. The bowling ball lands on the trampoline, which stretches downward until the ball stops, just barely before touching the ground. Sketch an energy bar chart of the situation. What is the elastic spring constant of the trampoline fabric?

6. A friend stands in a treehouse 5.55 m off the ground. She drops a bowling ball of mass 6.00 kg onto a highly elastic trampoline 2.89 m above the ground. The bowling ball lands on the trampoline, which stretches downward until the ball stops, just barely before touching the ground. What is the elastic spring constant of the trampoline fabric?

a. 13.4 N/m   **b.** 22.6 N/m

c. 73.7 N/m   **d.** 78.1 N/m

Conservation of Energy

The law of conservation of energy states that energy is neither created nor destroyed. For this to remain true, any change in the internal energy in a system indicates that work was done on the system.

Conservation of Energy
$$E_i + W = E_f$$
E_i = initial energy of the system
W = net work done on the system
E_f = final energy of the system

Systems are either open or closed. A closed system can exchange energy but not matter with its surroundings. The total energy of a closed system is constant. Any change in a specific type of energy requires an equivalent change in another form of energy present in the system.

You can use the conservation of energy to equate the total energy of a closed system at two different points in time.

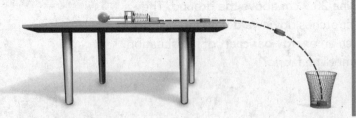

Energy Transformations The puck-spring-Earth system shown is a closed system.

The potential energy stored in the spring and in Earth's gravitational field is transformed into the kinetic energy of the puck.

No external work is done on the system.

An open system can exchange both matter and energy with its surroundings. The total energy of an open system changes when work is done on or by the system. Open systems can be represented by an expanded version of the work-energy theorem.

Expanded Work-Energy Theorem
$$KE_i + PE_{gi} + PE_{si} + W = KE_f + PE_{gf} + PE_{sf}$$
KE_i, KE_f = initial/final kinetic energy
PE_{gi}, PE_{gf} = initial/final gravitational potential energy
PE_{si}, PE_{sf} = initial/final elastic potential energy
W = net work done on the system

Define the Problem Why are the spring, puck, and Earth each included when defining the system shown in the diagram while the table is not?

_____

_____

_____

Mathematical Practices: Make Sense of Problems

Many mechanical systems are composed of several subsystems. When solving mechanical problems, you must first define the system of interest and evaluate whether it is a closed or open system so that you can apply the conservation of energy and the work-energy theorem correctly.

Consider a motorcycle that slows to a stop when its brakes are applied.

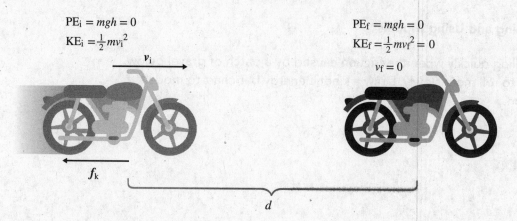

$$PE_i = mgh = 0$$
$$KE_i = \frac{1}{2}mv_i^2$$

v_i

f_k

d

$$PE_f = mgh = 0$$
$$KE_f = \frac{1}{2}mv_f^2 = 0$$

$v_f = 0$

When the **motorcycle** alone is defined as the system:
- the system is open
- external work is done on the system (friction from the pavement does work on the motorcycle)
- energy is not conserved in the system ($KE_i + PE_i > KE_f + PE_f$)

When the **motorcycle and pavement** together are defined as the system:
- the system is closed (and isolated)
- work is only done within the system (friction from the pavement does work on the motorcycle)
- $W = \Delta U_{int} = f_k d$
- energy is conserved in the system ($KE_i + PE_i = f_k d + KE_f + PE_f$)

3-Dimensional Review

1. DCI Definitions of Energy Based on the law of conservation of energy, if the final energy of a system is less than the initial energy of a system, what do we know about the system?

_____

_____

2. SEP Developing and Using Models

a. A ball is rolling quickly when the friction caused by a patch of gravel below it causes it to roll more slowly. Draw a kinetic energy bar chart to model the situation.

✏️

b. Is the system above open, closed, or isolated? Explain your answer.

_____

_____

c. If the ball from part A was initially starting on the side of a hill and then rolled to the bottom of the hill with the same slower final velocity, how would this impact the bar chart?

_____

_____

_____

3. CCC Energy and Matter Which of the following scenarios is an example of a system that can exchange both matter and energy with its surroundings? Circle all that apply.

a. hot coffee in a insulated flask

b. a beaker full of boiling water

c. soup heating in an uncovered pot on a stove

d. a bottle of water with the cap on

Skills Practice

4. A 980-kg roller coaster car drops from rest at a height of 70.5 m along a frictionless track. What is the velocity of the roller coaster at the top of a second hill that is 40.0 m high? What average force is required to bring the car to a stop along a 110 m stretch of horizontal track at ground level at the end of the ride?

5. A 750-kg roller coaster car drops from rest at a height of 130.0 m along a frictionless track. What is the velocity of the car at the top of a second hill that is 80.5 m high? What average force is required to bring the car to a stop along a 140 m stretch of horizontal track at ground level at the end of the ride?

6. An 860-kg roller coaster car drops from rest at a height of 184.0 m along a frictionless track. What average force is required to bring the car to a stop along a 180 m stretch of horizontal track at 1.4 m above the ground at the end of the ride?

a. 8620 N

b. 8600 N

c. 8700 N

d. 8800 N

Momentum and Impulse

Linear momentum (p) is the product of the mass (m) and velocity (v) of a moving object, or $p = mv$. Since momentum is dependent on velocity, it is defined for a particular frame of reference. Momentum is also a vector quantity, so it can be broken into x, y, and z components using vector reasoning. When multiple objects are in a system, their momenta add to give the total momentum. The diagram shows how vector addition may be used to find the total momentum of objects in the rocket system.

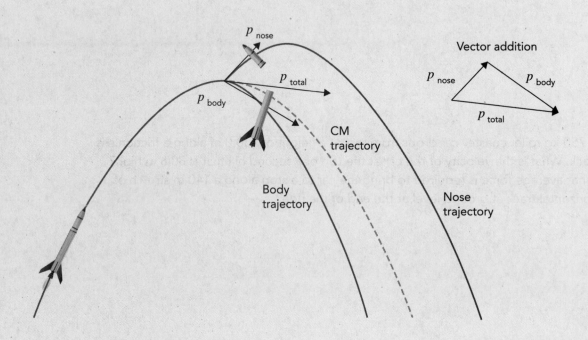

Rotating objects have angular momentum (L). Like objects moving along the ground, rotating objects have inertia due to mass, which is measured as the moment of inertia (I). The moment of inertia depends on how mass is distributed around the axis of rotation. The farther mass is distributed from the axis, the greater the moment of inertia. Angular momentum is the product of the moment of inertia and the angular velocity (ω), or $L = I\omega$.

When a net force is applied to an object in motion, its momentum changes. How rapidly the momentum changes depends on the time interval the force is applied. Therefore, it is useful to work with a quantity called impulse (J). Impulse is the product of the average force and the time interval over which the force is applied: $J = F_{avg}\Delta t$. In the same way, a torque exerted for a certain amount of time changes angular momentum: $\Delta L = \tau \Delta t$.

Use Mathematics Write an equation to find the magnitude of the total momentum of the objects in the rocket system.

Mathematical Practices: Make Sense of Problems

Drawing a picture and using vector reasoning are helpful strategies when solving momentum problems.

Sample Problem

A catapult fires a 50 kg boulder at a castle wall at a 45° angle. The initial velocity of the boulder when it leaves the catapult is 30 m/s. The boulder collides with the castle wall at the peak of its trajectory. If the collision of the boulder with the castle wall takes 0.8 seconds, what force is applied to the castle wall?

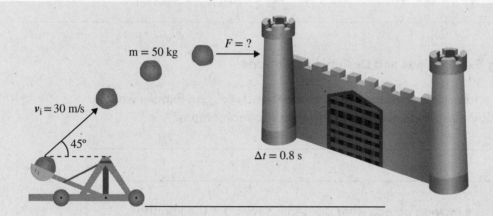

Draw a Picture

Drawing a labeled picture will help you identify knowns and unknowns. In this problem, it also helps you recognize that the boulder follows a projectile trajectory.

Use Vector Reasoning

At its peak height, the vertical component of velocity will equal zero. Only the horizontal component of velocity will contribute to the momentum of the boulder. Since momentum is a vector quantity, it can be broken into vector components just like velocity can.

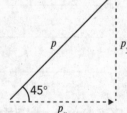

The total momentum of the boulder when it leaves the catapult is:

$p = mv = 50 \text{ kg} \cdot 30 \text{ m/s} = 1500 \text{ kg·m/s}$

To find the horizontal component of the total momentum:

$p_x = (1500 \text{ kg·m/s})(\cos 45°) = 1061 \text{ kg·m/s}$

Find the Impulse

An impulse will change the momentum of the boulder, so $J = \Delta p_x$. The force the boulder exerts on the castle wall will be equal and opposite to the impulse force.

$$F_{avg} \Delta t = \Delta p_x$$
$$F_{avg} = \frac{\Delta p_x}{\Delta t} = \frac{1061 \text{ kg·m/s}}{0.8 \text{ s}} = 1326 \text{ N}$$

3-Dimensional Review

1. DCI Forces and Motion Describe, in your own words, the relationship between linear momentum, moment of inertia, and angular momentum.

_____

_____

_____

_____

_____

2. SEP Constructing Explanations and Designing Solutions

  a. The impulse of a force can be found with the equation $J = F_{avg}\Delta t$. Explain what this means in your own words. How does this relate to momentum?

_____

_____

  b. If a collision stops a moving object, what does that say about the impulse?

_____

_____

  c. Engineers designing a car check its safety by performing a crash test. How can they minimize the impact force during the collision?

_____

_____

_____

3. CCC Cause and Effect A team is designing a truck. Which of the following adjustments will increase the momentum of the truck when it is in motion? Circle all that apply.

  a. increase the potential velocity of the truck

  b. decrease the potential velocity of the truck

  c. increase the mass of the truck

  d. decrease the mass of the truck

Skills Practice

4. A player kicks a 0.412-kg ball at a net that launches it at a 42.3° angle. The initial velocity of the ball is 13.4 m/s. The ball collides with the net's upper post at the peak of its trajectory. If the collision of the ball with the post takes 0.56 seconds, what force is applied to the post?

🖉

5. A 0.02-kg top spins in a circle 10.2 cm wide. The linear velocity of the top is 2.41 m/s and it leans at an angle of 87.7°. What is the angular momentum of the top?

🖉

6. A T-shirt cannon launches a 0.192-kg shirt into the stands at a sports arena. It launches the shirt at a 75.7° angle. The initial velocity of the shirt as it leaves the cannon is 34.8 m/s. The shirt is grabbed by a fan at the peak of its trajectory. If the force applied to the person grabbing the shirt is 1.31 N, how long was the shirt in flight?

a. 1.26 seconds

b. 2.16 seconds

c. 4.19 seconds

d. 8.87 seconds

Conservation of Momentum

The law of conservation of linear momentum states that if no external force acts on a system of particles or objects, the total linear momentum of the system does not change. This means that when a system is isolated, any interactions between objects within the system do not change the total momentum. In the same way, the law of conservation of angular momentum states that if a rotating system is isolated, the angular momentum of the system remains constant.

When external forces or torques are acting on objects within a system, the system is no longer isolated and the momentum of one or more objects will change. The impulse-momentum theorem applies. It states that the change in momentum of a system is equal to the net external impulse acting on it. How you define a system will determine whether or not it is isolated and whether or not you can expect the momentum of the system to change due to a net impulse.

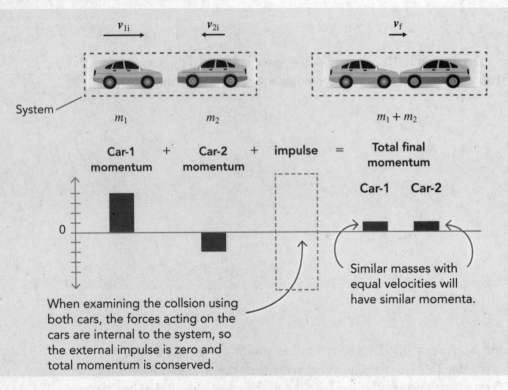

For an isolated system like the one shown above, the kinetic energy of the objects involved in the collision can change even though the total momentum remains constant. Kinetic energy can be transferred between objects during elastic collisions or it can be transformed into sound energy, thermal energy, or work during inelastic collisions.

Use Models According to the energy bar chart, how would you describe the motion of the cars after the collision?

_____

_____

Mathematical Practices: Model with Mathematics

Modeling changes in momentum and impulse using an energy bar chart is helpful when solving collision problems. To use the energy bar chart effectively, you need to identify which objects are part of the system and designate the positive and negative directions.

Sample Problem

An automotive engineer is testing different car bumpers at a crash test facility. During the test, the velocity of the test car (mass = 2500 kg) decreases from 20 m/s to 5 m/s. What is the average impact force if the time it takes the bumper to crumple is 0.4 s?

Using a Momentum Bar Chart

Consider how a bar chart can represent this situation.

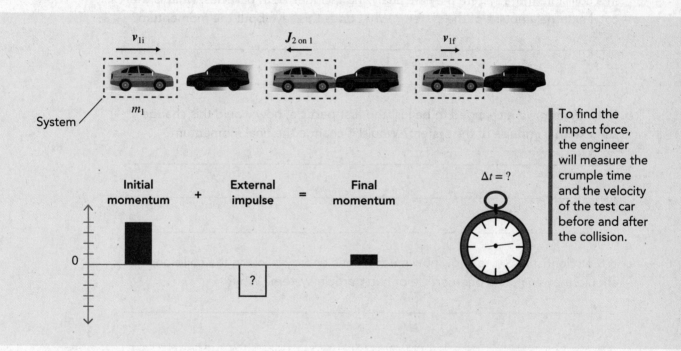

To find the impact force, the engineer will measure the crumple time and the velocity of the test car before and after the collision.

Because the engineer is interested in the impact force on the test car, the engineer defines the system as including one car only. The engineer also assigns the test car's forward direction as the positive direction. This means the impulse provided by the red car is external to the system and it is negative.

The engineer can use the bar chart model to construct an equation for the collision. The equation can be solved to find the average impact force, or $F_{2 \text{ on } 1}$.

Solution

$$m_1 v_{1i} + (-F_{2 \text{ on } 1}\Delta t) = m_1 v_{1f}$$

$$F_{2 \text{ on } 1} = -\frac{(m_1 v_{1f} - m_1 v_{1i})}{\Delta t}$$

$$F_{2 \text{ on } 1} = -\frac{[(2500 \text{ kg})(5 \text{ m/s}) - (2500 \text{ kg})(20 \text{ m/s})]}{0.4 \text{ s}} = 93,750 \text{ N}$$

3-Dimensional Review

1. DCI Forces and Motion In your own words, describe the law of conservation of linear momentum and how it relates to Newton's second and third laws of motion.

_____

_____

_____

_____

2. SEP Constructing Explanations and Designing Solutions

a. Scientists are testing particle collisions in the lab. Two particles come together in a collision. If the system they are analyzing includes both particles, what is the total external impulse of the system? What does this say about the momentum?

_____

_____

b. If the system were changed to be just the first particle, how would this change the external impulse of the system? Would it change the final momentum?

_____

_____

_____

c. If the scientists want to know how much kinetic energy is lost in the collision, should they analyze a one-particle or two-particle system? Why?

_____

_____

_____

3. CCC Cause and Effect Fill in the blanks. A _____ system of a totally _____ car collision will result in the largest external impulse.

a. 2-car; inelastic   **b.** 2-car; elastic

c. 1-car; inelastic   **d.** 1-car; elastic

Skills Practice

4. A tennis player serves a 0.058-kg ball at 62.2 m/s. The opposing player returns the ball to the server at 67.4 m/s. If the ball was in contact with the opposing player's racket for 5.51 ms, determine the average force the tennis racket exerted on the tennis ball. Draw a momentum-impulse bar chart to help your work.

5. A 1610-kg truck traveling east at 24 m/s collides with a 1080-kg car traveling south at 14 m/s. After the collision, the vehicles do not separate. Determine the x- and y-components of the velocity of the combined vehicles immediately after the collision. Draw momentum-impulse bar charts for the x- and y-direction to help your work.

6. In a ballistic pendulum, a pellet with a mass of 0.040 kg is fired with an initial speed of 28 m/s at a pendulum block that is at rest. The block has a mass of 1.8 kg and is suspended from a rod of length 0.28 m. After the pellet collides with the block, they both stick together and swing upward. Determine the maximum height reached by the pellet-and-block system.

a. 0.019 m

b. 0.034 m

c. 0.13 m

d. 0.28 m

Collisions in Earth's Crust

Earth's surface layer, the lithosphere, is a system of oceanic and continental plates. The churning mantle beneath the lithosphere causes the plates to move at different rates and in different directions.. The shifting plates collide, separate, or slide past each other. The system of plate motions on Earth's surface is called plate tectonics.

Interactions between lithospheric plates result in stress forces that can compress, extend, or bend rock. To relieve strain, rock can break and snap back in an earthquake. Faulting and buckling may also occur. Deformation is usually greatest at plate boundaries.

The surface features of Earth are the result of tectonic forces. Scientists observe patterns in the types of features that appear near convergent, divergent, and transform boundaries. They use these patterns to help reconstruct a geologic history of Earth.

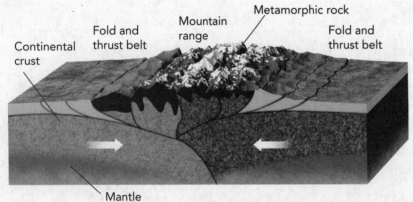

When two continental plates collide, the plate with the higher density will subduct (sink) below the other. Compression forces where the plates meet will cause the rock to fold and thrust upward.

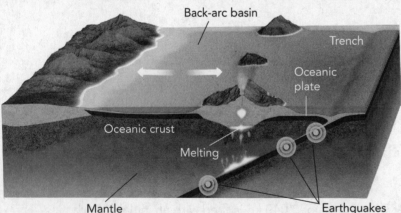

When two oceanic plates collide, subduction of one plate under the other will cause a deep ocean trench to form. Hot magma can push up through the overriding plate, forming volcanoes and an island arc.

Identify Patterns Most mountain ranges have rows of mountain peaks. Will the mountain rows be parallel or perpendicular to the colliding plate boundary? Why?

_____

_____

_____

Science Practices: Developing Models

Modeling allows scientists to represent changes in the Earth system over very short or very long periods of time. They develop models to explain forces that shape Earth's surface, to make predictions about how Earth's surface might change in the future, and to hypothesize how Earth's surface looked in the past. Modeling is one process that scientists use to construct a geologic history of Earth.

Consider how models can have different goals and how they represent change in the Earth system over different periods of time. Maps that show the location and type of plate boundaries in a particular geographic region represent the present time only. They are useful for connecting surface features with plate tectonics in that region.

Other models show change over very long periods of time. The series of diagrams to the right shows the Wilson cycle, the opening and closing of ocean basins through a series of stages over at least 0.5 billion years. The goal of the model is to show the forces, plate movements, and land features associated with each stage of the cycle.

Models can have multiple uses. In addition to showing stages of a process, the Wilson cycle model might be used to construct geologic histories for different locations on Earth. If movement data is added to a map that shows the location of plate boundaries, it may give scientists some indication of where stress is building in the Earth system.

Stage	Motion
Embryonic	Uplift (rifting)
Juvenile	Divergence (subsidence)
Mature	Divergence (spreading)
Complex	Divergence and convergence (spreading and subduction)
Terminal	Convergence (collision and uplift)
Suturing	Convergence (horizontal shrinkage)

3-Dimensional Review

1. **DCI Earth Materials and Systems** How does the collision of Earth's tectonic plates cause divergent boundaries, convergent boundaries, and transform boundaries? In what type of boundary does strike-slip faulting occur? Explain your answer.

_____

_____

_____

2. **SEP Developing and Using Models**

   a. Refer to the series of diagrams that model the Wilson cycle. The Mediterranean Sea is currently in the terminal stage of the cycle. What can be concluded about the current size of the Mediterranean Sea?

   _____

   _____

   _____

   b. Compare the movement of continents during the juvenile and suturing stages of the Wilson cycle. Explain your answer.

   _____

   _____

   c. Explain the processes that occur in the complex stage of the Wilson cycle and the natural phenomena that occur as a result.

   _____

   _____

   _____

   _____

3. **CCC Stability and Change** Scientists notice the following changes at a certain location: earthquakes, a new mountain forming, volcanic eruption along a ridge. What is the likely cause of these changes?

   a. a mid-ocean ridge at a divergent boundary

   b. a subduction zone at a convergent boundary

   c. a continent-continent collision at a convergent boundary

   d. a geological fault at a transform boundary

Skills Practice

4. Draw a model that shows the vertical stress forces and horizontal stress forces for a normal fault. Label the forces and direction of forces in the model.

5. Draw a model of an earthquake at a divergent boundary. Include the mantle, oceanic crust, and direction of plate movement.

6. According to the Wilson cycle model, which of the following could be estimated by the occurrence of a narrow sea with two geographically similar coastlines? Circle all that apply.

a. The sea is likely to be relatively young.

b. The sea is likely the location of a strike-slip fault.

c. The sea likely has a divergence occurring.

d. The sea likely has a complex, subduction zone.

Temperature

An object can gain energy through heating or by having work done on it. The first law of thermodynamics states that a change in a system's internal energy, ΔU_{int}, is equal to the amount of work, W, done on the system plus the amount of energy transferred into the system through heating, Q. The first law may be expressed in the following equation.

First Law of Thermodynamics

$$W + Q = \Delta U_{int}$$

ΔU_{int} = change in internal energy

W = work done on the system

Q = energy transferred through heating

In a thermodynamic process, thermal energy moves through a system due to energy transfer or changes in pressure, volume, or temperature. Some examples of thermodynamic processes include melting ice (and other phase changes), heating a pot on a stove, cooling food in a refrigerator, or using an expanding gas to push a piston. Not all thermodynamic processes involve a change in internal energy.

Thermodynamic Processes

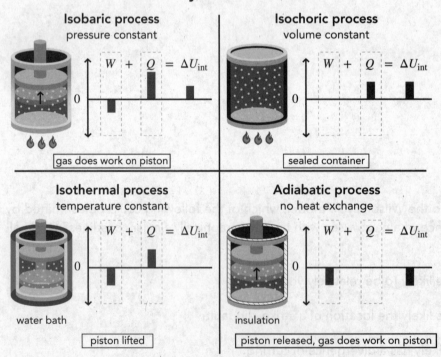

Isobaric process
pressure constant
$W + Q = \Delta U_{int}$
gas does work on piston

Isochoric process
volume constant
$W + Q = \Delta U_{int}$
sealed container

Isothermal process
temperature constant
$W + Q = \Delta U_{int}$
water bath
piston lifted

Adiabatic process
no heat exchange
$W + Q = \Delta U_{int}$
insulation
piston released, gas does work on piston

Use Models Look at the diagram for the isobaric process. Describe the energy conservation in this system.

_____

_____

Mathematical Practices: Model with Mathematics

Modeling thermodynamic processes using pressure-volume graphs and energy bar charts helps you to evaluate how work and heat are affecting the internal energy of a system.

The diagram below shows that an external force is used to compress a gas. The thermometers show that the temperature does not change.

What must happen to the system to keep the temperature constant?

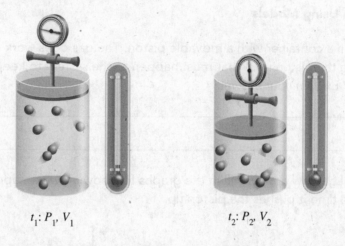

$t_1: P_1, V_1$ $t_2: P_2, V_2$

Assume the ideal gas law applies. If the temperature remains constant, the pressure must increase as the volume decreases. The particles move with the same kinetic energy so they collide more frequently with the sides of the container.

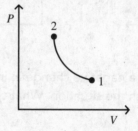

Since an external force is applied to the piston, work is done on the gas.

The internal energy of a system is dependent on temperature, so if temperature is constant, this is an **isothermal system** and $\Delta U_{int} = 0$.

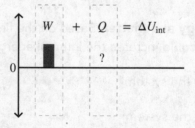

To satisfy the first law of thermodynamics, heat must be removed from the gas to maintain the constant temperature. In an isothermal system, this happens through energy exchange with the surroundings.

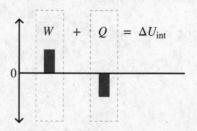

3-Dimensional Review

1. DCI Definitions of Energy What properties of particles relate to kinetic energy? How does this relate to temperature?

_____

_____

_____

2. SEP Developing and Using Models

a. A gas is enclosed in a container with a movable piston. The gas does work on the piston, pushing the piston up. What must happen to the system to keep the pressure constant? Explain your answer.

_____

_____

b. Assuming the ideal gas law applies, fill in the graphs for showing what happens to the gas over the time it pushes the piston up.

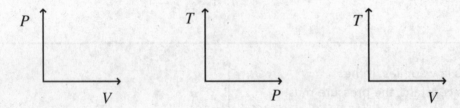

c. If the system has a negative change in internal energy, fill in the chart to match the situation. What type of system does this represent?

_____

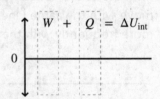

3. CCC Energy and Matter Based on the first law of thermodynamics, which of the following could increase the internal energy of a system. Circle all that apply.

a. heating the system

b. cooling the system

c. doing work on the system

d. work done by the system

Skills Practice

4. A volume of an ideal gas is enclosed in a container with a movable piston. During a process, the gas expands as the pressure decreases. Temperature is held constant. Sketch a pressure-volume graph of the situation. Then determine what type of process this is and sketch an energy bar chart of the situation.

5. A volume of an ideal gas is enclosed in a container with a movable piston. During a process, the gas has a constant volume while the pressure increases. Sketch a pressure-volume graph of the situation. Then determine what type of process this is and sketch an energy bar chart of the situation.

6. A volume of an ideal gas is enclosed in a container with a movable piston. During a process, the gas expands as the pressure remains constant. What is the resulting internal energy of the system?

a. $\Delta U_{int} = 0$ **b.** $\Delta U_{int} = W$

c. $\Delta U_{int} = Q$ **d.** $\Delta U_{int} = W + Q$

Thermal Equilibrium and Heat Flow

The second law of thermodynamics states that the net change in entropy of a system and its environment must always be greater than zero. Entropy (S) is a measure of disorder. The second law is at work when materials at different temperatures are in contact and heat flows between them until they reach thermal equilibrium. As thermal energy transfers from the warmer material to the colder material, the system including the two materials becomes more disordered over time. The entropy of the system increases. Thermal energy can transfer between materials by conduction, convection, or radiation.

Many engineered devices take advantage of the heat flow described by the second law. Heat engines use the transfer of thermal energy to do mechanical work. In comparison, heat pumps use work to transfer thermal energy. Engineers strive to improve the efficiency of heat engines by minimizing the transfer of thermal energy to the surroundings. They try to improve the performance of heat pumps by minimizing the work needed to transfer thermal energy between hot and cold reservoirs.

Efficiency of a Heat Engine	Performance Coefficient of a Heat Pump
$$e = \left\lvert \frac{W}{Q_H} \right\rvert$$	$$K = \left\lvert \frac{Q_H}{W} \right\rvert$$
e = efficiency of engine W = work done by system Q_H = thermal energy absorbed by system	K = thermal performance coefficient Q_H = thermal energy added to hot reservoir W = work done on the system

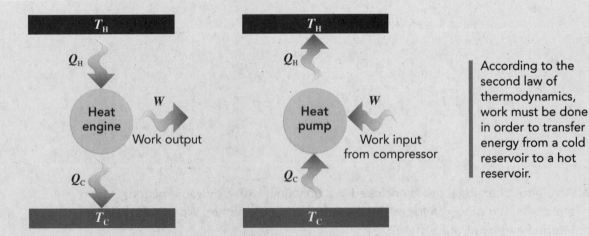

According to the second law of thermodynamics, work must be done in order to transfer energy from a cold reservoir to a hot reservoir.

Calculate A heat engine provides 18,500 J of work when 22,600 J of thermal energy are transferred from the hot reservoir. What is the efficiency of the heat engine?

Mathematical Practices: Model with Mathematics

Energy bar charts and equations are useful for evaluating the performance of technologies that transfer thermal energy. Consider how they might be used to compare the performance of a heat pump design before and after it is optimized to improve efficiency. In this case, optimization of the design allows more thermal energy to transfer to the cold reservoir for the same amount of work.

Before Optimization

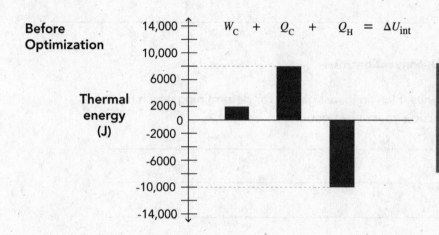

The performance coefficient compares the thermal energy transferred from the hot reservoir to the work required.

$$K = \left|\frac{Q_H}{W}\right| = \left|\frac{-10{,}000\ \text{J}}{2000\ \text{J}}\right| = 5$$

After Optimization

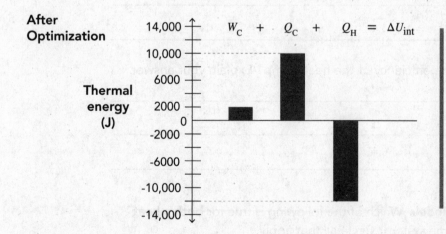

After optimization, the performance coefficient increases.

$$K = \left|\frac{Q_H}{W}\right| = \left|\frac{-12{,}000\ \text{J}}{2000\ \text{J}}\right| = 6$$

One way that engineers might drive more thermal energy into a working refrigerant is to increase the surface area available for energy transfer.

These energy bar charts align with the first and second laws of thermodynamics. Energy must be conserved in a heat pump so there is no net gain or loss of energy from the system. The heat flow from a warm to cold reservoir in the heat pump cannot take place without work input.

3-Dimensional Review

1. DCI Conservation of Energy and Energy Transfer According to the second law of thermodynamics, what happens to energy and entropy when a cold object comes into contact with a warmer one?

_____

_____

_____

_____

2. SEP Planning and Carrying Out Investigations

a. You are given two heat engines. Plan an investigation for determining which heat pump is more efficient. Describe your investigation.

_____

_____

_____

b. How might your investigation change if you were given two heat pumps instead?

_____

_____

_____

c. How might you increase the efficiency of the heat pump? Explain your answer.

_____

_____

_____

3. CCC Systems and System Models Which of the following is true for **both** a heat engine system and a heat pump system? Circle all that apply.

a. Energy is conserved in the system.

b. Entropy increases as a result of the system.

c. Work is done by the system.

d. Temperature of the system will increase.

Skills Practice

4. During one cycle, the engine of a lawn tractor absorbs 418 J of thermal energy and exhausts 136 J of thermal energy. Draw an energy bar chart of the situation and determine the efficiency of the heat engine.

5. During one cycle, the engine of a lawn tractor absorbs 341 J of thermal energy and exhausts 86 J of thermal energy. Draw an energy bar chart of the situation and determine the efficiency of the heat engine.

6. During one cycle, the engine of a lawn tractor absorbs 502 J of thermal energy and exhausts 117 J of thermal energy. What is the efficiency of the heat engine?

a. 23.3%

b. 47.7%

c. 68.4%

d. 76.7%

Heat Flow Within Earth

Scientists use seismic waves to understand the interior layers of Earth. The speed, refraction, and diffraction of P and S waves provide information about the temperature, density, and depth of each layer. The data reveal that Earth's outer core is liquid iron while the mantle is molten rock.

Heat within Earth has multiple sources: heat from when the planet formed, heat due to adiabatic compression, and heat from the decay of radioactive elements. Thermal energy transfer from Earth's center causes convection cells in the outer core and mantle. The flow of matter in the mantle causes the movement of tectonic plates and the flow of matter in the outer core generates Earth's magnetic field.

Conduction, Convection, and Radiation Within Earth

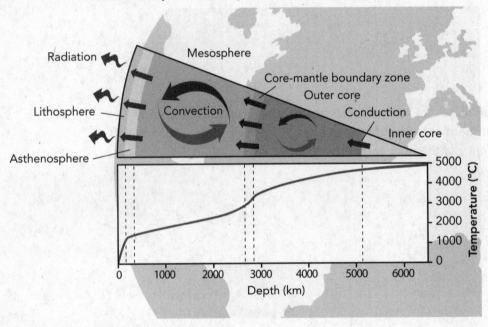

The two largest temperature changes occur at the thermal boundary layers of the lithosphere and the core-mantle boundary zone.

Use Graphs Use evidence from the graph to explain the movement of matter and energy through the mesosphere.

_____

_____

_____

_____

_____

_____

Science Practices: Construct Explanations

The data that scientists collect about temperatures and heat transfer in Earth's interior help to explain features and changes at Earth's surface. Models are useful tools when using data to construct explanations about what causes various geologic phenomena. The model below explains the formation of some of Earth's surface features.

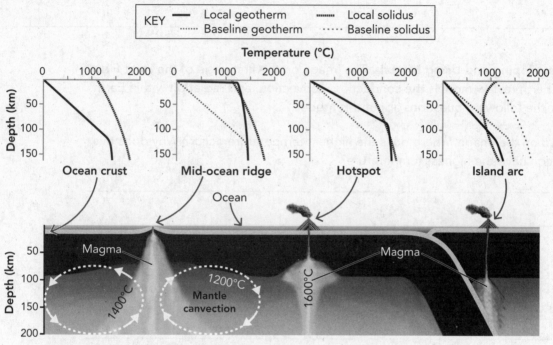

Graphs by Woudloper/Woodwalker, licensed under CC BY 4.0 International Public License. Savvas Learning Company modified the material.

Consider how the diagram and graphs work together to explain the formation of mid-oceanic ridges, volcanoes, and island arcs.

- Layers of Earth are represented by different colors in the diagram.
- Arrows show the movement of matter due to convection in Earth's mantle, which cause drag forces that act on the crustal plates above.
- Temperature labels reveal that plumes of magma at 1400°C and 1600°C rise upward in cooler regions of the mantle (1200°C).
- Temperature graphs show that magma forms where the local geotherm is at a higher temperature than the local solidus.
- Raised features at Earth's surface show new rock formation where magma breaks through the ocean crust (mid-oceanic ridge and volcanoes); viewers can infer that more rock accretion occurs when magma is at a higher temperature.

Constructing explanations about the formation of Earth's magnetic field is more difficult because the convection currents in the outer core are more complex than those in the mantle and there is less data available. Scientists use computer modeling to help construct these explanations because computers can generate 3D images that account for the variability in the core's convection currents.

3-Dimensional Review

1. DCI Earth Materials and Systems Describe, in your own words, the three outer layers of Earth.

_____

_____

_____

_____

2. SEP Developing and Using Models The image on the first page of the Heat Flow Within Earth review models the conduction, convection, and radiation within Earth. Answer the following questions about this model.

a. Based on the image, where does the highest temperature occur? Why does this location have the highest temperature?

_____

_____

_____

b. What is the approximate temperature difference between the outer core and the inner core?

_____

c. Earth's core was entirely molten for most of its history. Now, how many parts does the core have? How could scientists tell the difference between these parts?

_____

_____

_____

3. CCC Energy and Matter Which of the following is a main source of Earth's interior energy? Circle all that apply.

a. thermal energy provided by the sun's rays

b. adiabatic compression

c. resulting energy from Earth's formation

d. heat radiation at Earth's crust

Skills Practice

4. Use one of the models on the previous pages to explain how the flow of matter in the mantle causes the crustal plates to move. Explain why you chose that model.

_____

_____

_____

_____

_____

_____

5. In the liquid iron of the outer core, convection takes place vigorously, generating Earth's magnetic field. Draw a model of Earth's magnetic field, include Earth's axis for reference.

6. Which of the following can be explained by the Temperature and Depth model shown under Science Practices?

a. heat conduction through stone and metal

b. how subduction zones form magma

c. how Earth's magnetic field is formed

d. the sources of Earth's energy

Electric Potential

A charged particle or object (called the source charge) is surrounded by an energy field. If the potential energy (PE_q) of a test charge (q) in that field is known, the electric potential (V) may be found using this equation: $V = \frac{PE_q}{q}$.

It is useful to think of an ideal charge as being just a single point. Electric potential due to a point charge depends on the magnitude of the source charge (q) and the distance from the source charge (r). Electric potential is a scalar quantity, which means that the total electric potential on a test charge will equal the sum of all fields interacting at the test charge's location.

Potential Field of a Point Charge
$$V = k_e \frac{q}{r}$$
V = electric potential k_e = Coulomb's constant = 8.99×10^9 N·m²/C² q = source charge r = distance

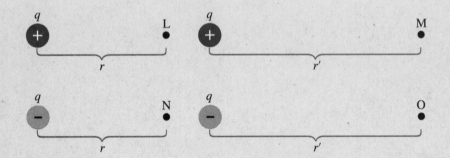

The potential at point M is less than at point L. The potential at point O is less than at point N. Remember: When a negative potential decreases, the numerical value becomes less negative (example: –10 V to –5 V).

Potential energy converts to kinetic energy as a charge accelerates through an electric field. If the charge passes through an electrical device, its potential energy can also be converted into other energy forms, such as heat, sound or light.

An equipotential surface is a surface that has the same electric potential everywhere. If a charge is placed between surfaces with different potentials, it will experience a force. The potential difference (ΔV) between the surfaces (a and b) can be found by subtracting their electric potentials: $\Delta V = V_a - V_b$.

Calculate What is the electric potential of a test charge that is 0.01 m from a 5.0 C sphere?

_____

_____

Mathematical Practices: Model with Mathematics

Force diagrams and energy bar charts are useful for tracking motion and energy transformations in systems involving charged objects. A system of like charges will have positive potential energy. A system of opposite charges will have negative potential energy.

The force diagrams show initial and final conditions for two opposite charges. The energy bar chart shows changes in electric potential energy and kinetic energy within the system. Notice that no external work is done because the system includes both charges.

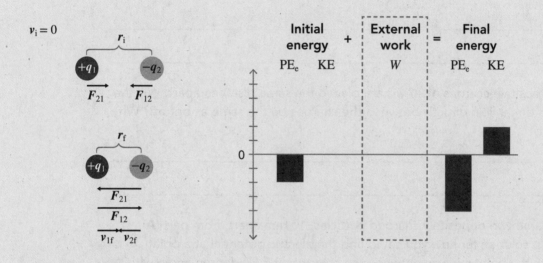

Using Force Diagrams

The force diagram uses vectors to represent the magnitude and direction of the forces acting on each charge. The diagram assumes that the two test charges have equal amounts of charge. For this reason, the forces acting on each charge are equal and opposite. As the distance (r) between the charges decreases, the electric potential at the location of each charge increases. The forces they exert on each other increase in magnitude. The notation F_{21} means "the force of charge 2 on charge 1." The charges are numbered from left to right in the diagram. The velocity vectors reveal that the charges are moving toward each other with equal speed.

Using Energy Bar Charts

The energy bar chart shows that the initial negative potential energy is less than the final negative potential energy because the charges are farther apart. As the charges accelerate toward each other, kinetic energy increases. Energy is conserved in the system. The increase in negative potential energy is offset by the positive change in kinetic energy.

3-Dimensional Review

1. DCI Definitions of Energy In your own words, describe what an electric potential field is and how it is related to electric potential.

_____

_____

2. SEP Constructing Explanations and Designing Solutions

    a. A positive charge of +7 μC and a negative charge of –7 μC are 10 mm apart. What is the electric potential field directly between the charges? Explain your answer.

    _____

    _____

    b. Now, two positive charges of +7 μC are placed the same distance apart. Will the electric potential field directly between the charges be the same as before? Why or why not?

    _____

    _____

    c. Take the same two oppositely charged particles, 10 mm apart, from part (A). Construct a solution for how you could find the electric potential at a point 11 cm from the point midway between the charges, at a 90-degree angle with the line segment connecting the two. Do not actually solve.

    _____

    _____

    _____

3. CCC Energy and Matter Which of the following scenarios will result in a final energy that is all positive potential energy?

    a. two positively charged particles experiencing electromagnetic force

    b. two oppositely charged particles experiencing electromagnetic force

    c. two negatively charged particles with a force inward equal to the electromagnetic force

    d. two oppositely charged particles with a force outward equal to the electromagnetic force

Skills Practice

4. During a transformation, a positive radon nucleus repels a positive helium nucleus ($m = 6.64 \times 10^{-27}$ kg), giving it an energy of 7.37×10^{-13} J. How fast is the helium nucleus moving when it is far away from the radon nucleus? Draw an energy bar chart to assist you.

5. A positive charge of $+7.2$ μC and a positive charge of $+6.64$ μC are 10 cm apart, at rest. After t seconds, the particles are at a distance 15 meters apart with velocities -8.7 m/s and 9.1 m/s, respectively. Draw an energy bar chart of the situation and determine the direction of the forces and velocities of each charge.

6. Two oppositely charged particles sit next to one another at rest and do not move. Which of the following **must** be true of the system?

a. It has a negative initial potential energy.

b. It has a positive initial potential energy.

c. There is external work being done.

d. It has a positive final potential energy.

Energy in Electric Circuits

Voltage is the electric potential difference that produces electric current between two points in a circuit. Resistance in a circuit is provided by any electrical device that draws energy from the current, converting it into other forms such as heat, light, sound, or motion. Ohm's law describes the relationship between voltage, current, and resistance. The power used across a device may be calculated using Joule's law.

Ohm's Law	Joule's Law
$$I = \frac{V}{R}$$	$$P = I^2 R = IV = \frac{V^2}{R}$$
I = current V = voltage R = resistance	P = power I = current R = resistance V = voltage

Circuits with only one path for current flow are called series circuits, while parallel circuits have more than one path for current flow. Circuit diagrams use a variety of symbols to model the resistances connected in series or in parallel to a source of voltage, such as a battery or a capacitor. Kirchhoff's rules describe conditions that must be met for each loop (path) in a circuit.

- **Kirchhoff's loop rule:** In a complete circuit, all of the decreases in potential from resistance and all of the increases in potential from electromotive force must sum to zero.

- **Kirchhoff's junction rule:** The sum of the currents entering a junction is equal to the sum of the currents leaving the junction.

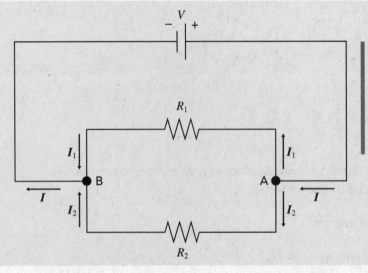

This is a parallel circuit because current can travel through resistor 1 (R_1) or resistor 2 (R_2).

According to the loop rule:
$V = I_1 R_1 + I_2 R_2$

According to the junction rule:
$I_{1A} + I_{2A} = I_{1B} + I_{2B} = I$

Apply Mathematical Concepts How should you modify the loop rule equation provided ($V = I_1R_1 + I_2R_2$) if a second voltage source (V_2) is added to the circuit before the parallel branches? Assume the new voltage source is oriented in the same direction as the original voltage source.

Mathematical Practices:
Look For and Make Use of Structure

You can make use of the loop structure of circuits to help you solve circuit problems. Consider the circuit shown.

This circuit has 2 loops. You can use Kirchhoff's loop rule to write an equation for each loop.

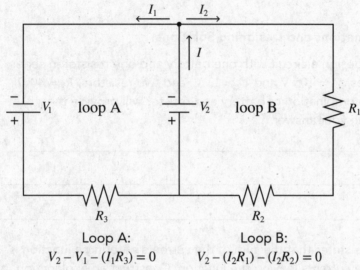

Loop A:
$$V_2 - V_1 - (I_1R_3) = 0$$

Loop B:
$$V_2 - (I_2R_1) - (I_2R_2) = 0$$

Notice that voltage 1 is subtracted from voltage 2 in the equation for loop A because the voltage sources are oriented in opposite directions within the loop.

You can use Kirchhoff's junction rule to write an equation for current. The total current (I) divides into I_1 and I_2, or $I = I_1 + I_2$

You can use these equations to solve for specific quantities.

Sample Problem
Suppose all of the resistors in the circuit shown are 100 Ω. The two batteries provide different voltages. Voltmeter measurements show that $V_1 = 6$ V and $V_2 = 12$ V. What are I, I_1, and I_2?

Step 1 Use the equation for loop A to find I_1

$$V_2 - V_1 - (I_1R_3) = 0$$

$$12 \text{ V} - 6 \text{ V} - (I_1 \cdot 100 \text{ }\Omega) = 0$$

$$I_1 = \frac{6 \text{ V}}{100 \text{ }\Omega} = 0.06 \text{ A}$$

Step 2 Use the equation for loop B to find I_2

$$V_2 - (I_2R_1) - (I_2R_2) = 0$$

$$12 \text{ V} - (I_2 \cdot 100 \text{ }\Omega) - (I_2 \cdot 100 \text{ }\Omega) = 0$$

$$I_2 = \frac{12 \text{ V}}{200 \text{ }\Omega} = 0.06 \text{ A}$$

Step 3 Use the current equation to find the total current, I

$$I = I_1 + I_2 = 0.06 \text{ A} + 0.06 \text{ A} = 1.2 \text{ A}$$

3-Dimensional Review

1. DCI Definitions of Energy Explain, in your own words, how voltage, current, and resistance are related.

_____

_____

2. SEP Constructing Explanations and Designing Solutions

a. An engineer wants to design a circuit with one battery and one resistor in series. They have two batteries, $V_1 = 105$ V and $V_2 = 13$ V, and two resistors, $R_1 = 40\ \Omega$ and $R_2 = 3.2\ \Omega$. Which combination of battery and resistor will provide the highest current? Explain your answer.

_____

_____

_____

b. Kirchhoff's junction rule states that the sum of the currents entering a junction is equal to the sum of the currents leaving the junction. Construct an explanation for why this has to be true.

_____

_____

_____

_____

_____

c. A circuit is designed with a voltage source and two resistors in series. Write an equation that could be used to solve for the current in the circuit.

_____

3. CCC Energy and Matter Which of the following statements is true regarding the relationship between current, voltage, power, and resistance in a series circuit?

a. Current is inversely proportional to voltage.

b. Power is inversely proportional to voltage.

c. Resistance is directly proportional to current.

d. Resistance is directly proportional to voltage.

Skills Practice

4. For the circuit shown in the diagram, $V_1 = 6$ V, $V_2 = 8$ V, $V_3 = 10$ V, $R_1 = 4\ \Omega$, and $R_2 = 10\ \Omega$. Determine the direction and magnitude of the current through both resistors.

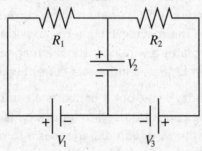

5. In the circuit shown, $V_1 = 18$ V, $V_2 = 13$ V, $V_3 = 16$ V, $R_1 = 14\ \Omega$, $R_2 = 12\ \Omega$, and $R_3 = 7.0\ \Omega$. Determine the direction and magnitude of the current through resistor 1.

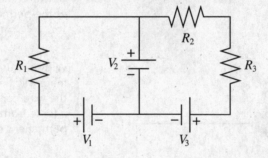

6. Using the same information and circuit in question 5, determine the direction and magnitude of the current through resistor 3.

a. 0.16 A clockwise

b. 0.16 A counterclockwise

c. 1.5 A clockwise

d. 1.5 A counterclockwise

Power Generation

An electric generator is a device that converts mechanical energy into electrical energy. Generators can produce direct current (DC) or alternating current (AC), and they operate according to Faraday's law. The mechanical energy provided from an external source, such as wind or water, rotates a wire coil within a magnetic field. The changing magnetic flux generates an EMF and induces a current within the coil.

A motor also operates according to Faraday's law, but it converts electrical energy into mechanical energy. Inside the motor, current is used to induce a magnetic field around a loop of wire. Each side of the wire loop experiences a torque from a permanent magnet. The torques cause the loop to rotate. Other devices, such as transformers and metal detectors, also use induction to convert energy from one form to another.

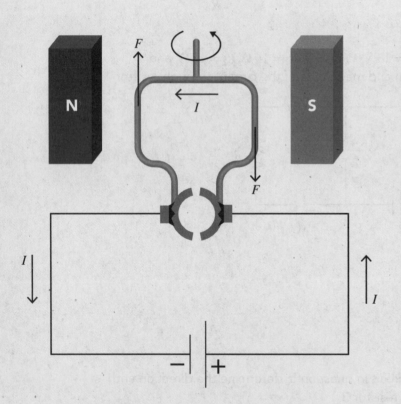

The energy to rotate the coil is provided by the strong magnetic field between the N and S poles of the permanent magnet.

Without current to generate a magnetic field through the coil, the wire coil will not experience a force from the field around the permanent magnet.

The current is possible because of the electrical potential energy stored in the voltage source. In a chemical battery, the potential energy is due to a potential difference between two equipotential surfaces.

Develop Models In the space provided, draw a flow chart to show the energy transformations that make the motor work.

Mathematical Practices: Make Sense of Problems

Mathematical problems related to generators and motors might require the use of Faraday's law, Ohm's law, Joule's law, and/or Kirchhoff's rules. Defining the problem by listing knowns and unknowns can help you determine which law(s) to apply to a specific problem.

Sample Problem

A wire coil inside a generator has 100 square loops and an area equal to 0.0036 m². The coil rotates one-quarter turn in 2.8 ms. If a 0.75 T magnetic field surrounds the coil, what is the maximum electromotive force induced in the coil?

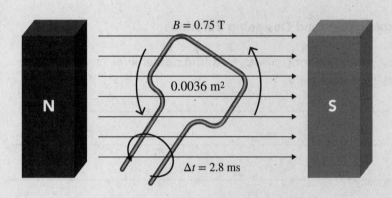

Step 1 Define the Problem

The known and unknown values provided in the problem include:

$N = 100$ loops

$A =$ area of loop $= 0.0036$ m²

$\Delta t = 2.8$ ms

$B = 0.75$ T

$V_E =$ induced EMF $= ?$

Step 2 Plan and Execute

By comparing the known variables to the available equations, you can choose an equation, or combination of equations, to solve for the unknown. The Faraday's law and magnetic flux equations match the known and unknown variables.

Faraday's law and Magnetic flux	$V_E = -N\frac{\Delta\Phi}{\Delta t}$ $\Delta\Phi = -BA$
Ohm's law	$I = \frac{V}{R}$
Joule's law	$P = I^2R = IV = \frac{V^2}{R}$

$$V_E = -N\frac{\Delta\Phi}{\Delta t} = N\frac{BA}{\Delta t}$$

$$V_E = 100 \text{ loops} \left(\frac{0.75 \text{ T} \cdot 0.0036 \text{ m}^2/\text{loop}}{0.0028 \text{ s}}\right) = 96 \text{ V}$$

Step 3 Evaluate

96 V seems reasonable when compared to the voltage provided by a typical household outlet, 120 V.

3-Dimensional Review

1. DCI Definitions of Energy What is the difference between AC and DC generators and how does this impact how they are used?

_____

_____

_____

_____

2. SEP Constructing Explanations and Designing Solutions

a. What type of device is used to bring power from the power lines to your home? Explain why this device is necessary.

_____

_____

_____

b. A simple motor uses just an energy source such as a battery and a wire loop in a magnetic field. Construct an explanation for how this creates mechanical energy.

_____

_____

c. If DC generators are used to power large electric motors and more sensitive devices, why are AC generators still employed?

_____

_____

3. CCC Energy and Matter Which of the following is true of electric motors? Circle all that apply.

a. Electric motors operate on the same principles as electric generators.

b. Electric motors transform electric energy into mechanical energy.

c. Motors can run on direct current only.

d. The forces of a magnetic field on electric current flowing through a coil cause the coil in a motor to rotate.

Skills Practice

4. A generator coil is rotated one quarter of a full revolution, from $\theta = 0°$ to $\theta = 90°$, in 13.2 ms. The coil has 353 loops, and it is a square 4.62 cm on a side. If the coil is in a uniform magnetic field of 0.991 T, what is the maximum electromotive force induced in the coil by the generator?

5. The coils in a motor have a resistance of 0.14 Ω and are driven by an EMF of 62 V. The back EMF induced in the motor is 37 V. Calculate the difference in power required by the motor at start up and at operating speed.

6. A wire coil inside a generator has 150 square loops and an area equal to 0.042 m². The coil rotates one-quarter turn in 1.7 ms. If a 0.86 T magnetic field surrounds the coil, what is the maximum electromotive force induced in the coil?

a. 3.2 V
b. 130 V

c. 1600 V
d. 3200 V

Energy Resources and Conservation

Several factors contribute to energy use: industrialization, human population growth, advances in technology, and the purchasing power of the average person (or affluence). Producing, storing, and using energy impacts biodiversity on Earth. Mathematical models, like the Ehrlich equation, provide a way to quantify the impact of energy use by a growing and advancing population.

Ehrlich Equation
$I = PAT$

I = impact A = affluence per person
P = human population T = technological efficiency

Energy use can be divided into four sectors: residential, commercial, industrial, and transportation. Managing the distribution of energy to these sectors must take into account changes in energy supply and energy demand over time. All forms of energy production involve costs and benefits, and the current rate of energy consumption is not sustainable. To plan for a sustainable future, human populations must develop solutions to maximize energy production while minimizing environmental impacts. Sustainable futures must also be economically viable and socially just.

How Energy Use Impacts Biodiversity

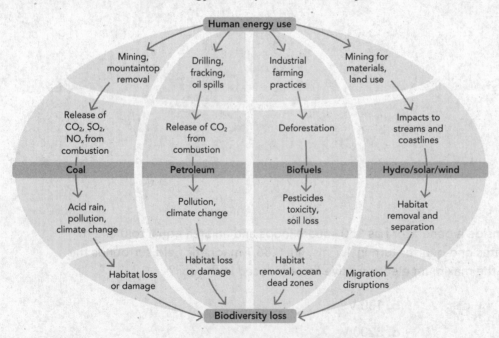

Compare Solutions Based on the information in the diagram, which types of energy are associated with the lowest levels of pollution?

Science Practices: Engaging in Argument from Evidence

Scientists engage in argumentation as they make claims about the costs and benefits of different types of energy production. There are several different measurements that they take into account: start-up costs; materials used; operation and maintenance costs; fuel costs; efficiency; waste disposal; land use and environmental impacts; storage requirements; energy produced per unit time; and utilization rates. Scientists make certain assumptions as they make comparisons, and these assumptions can have a large effect on the validity of an argument. So, when constructing arguments, scientists must be clear about what measurements they are taking into account and what assumptions they make.

The graph below presents the levelized costs of different energy sources over a nine-year period, from 2009 to 2018. The term "levelized" indicates that the energy types are compared on a per-unit basis (per megawatt hour) using annual averages. Costs shown are inflation-adjusted to 2017 values, and include construction, fuel, operations, and maintenance costs.

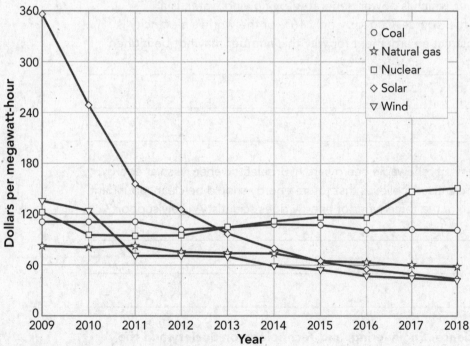

Levelized Cost of Energy Sources

Data source: Lazard's Levelized Cost of Energy, 2019

The arguments that scientists can make using this data are limited by the cost measurements included. Scientists can claim that the cost of solar energy production went down considerably over the nine-year period. They can also claim that the cost of wind energy decreased while other energy types changed more modestly, some increasing. However, scientists cannot use this data alone to claim that solar and wind energy are the best energy sources for a sustainable future because the data do not include environmental costs, social costs, or measurements related to energy supply and demand.

3-Dimensional Review

1. DCI Natural Resources A benefit of renewable energy sources is that they can be replaced and do not cause the levels of pollution that nonrenewable sources do. What are some of the costs of renewable resources?

_____

_____

_____

2. SEP Engaging in Argument from Evidence

  a. Fossil fuels continue to power most human activities because they release a great deal of energy when burned. However, economic costs of electricity from fossil fuels are now greater than for wind and solar power. Construct an argument for why this might be true.

_____

_____

  b. Hydroelectric power, which is power generated by flowing water, is a reliable and clean fuel source. Currently only 16% of the world's electricity is hydroelectric. Construct an argument for why this number may not be higher.

_____

_____

_____

  c. Three common forms of renewable energy are hydroelectric energy, solar energy, and wind energy. Scientist A believes that future energy should be clean, abundant, and low-cost. Which of the three types of energy does scientist A likely support?

_____

_____

_____

3. CCC Influence of Science, Engineering, and Technology on Society and the Natural World As scientists are looking for new energy sources to increase benefits while decreasing costs and risks, many have considered nuclear power. Which of the following is a **true** reason scientists might support nuclear power?

  a. Nuclear energy is a nonrenewable source.

  b. Nuclear fission power produces almost no greenhouse gases.

  c. Nuclear power is low in cost.

  d. Once atoms are split, they can continue to give more energy because they can be stored and split again.

Skills Practice

4. Based on the How Energy Use Impacts Biodiversity diagram, which of the energy resources release toxic pollutants into the environment?

_____

_____

_____

5. Based on the Ehrlich equation for sustainability, $I = PAT$, what variable is the easiest to affect for increasing sustainability?

_____

_____

_____

6. Based on the Levelized Cost of Energy Sources graph, what argument could scientists make about wind energy? Circle all that apply.

a. Wind energy is the best choice for a sustainable future.

b. Wind energy is currently a very cost-effective energy source.

c. Wind energy is trending to a decrease in cost.

d. Wind energy is the most efficient energy source.

Wave Properties

A mechanical wave is an oscillation of matter that is either perpendicular (transverse) or parallel (longitudinal) to the wave's direction. The speed a wave travels through a medium depends on the stiffness and density of the medium.

Speed of a Wave
$$v = f\lambda$$
where v is wave speed, f is frequency, and λ is wavelength

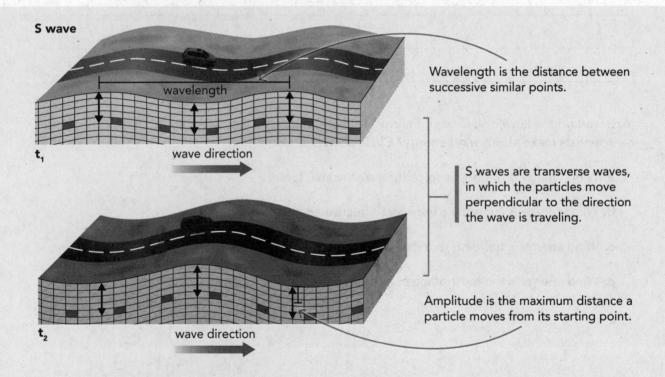

S wave

wavelength

t_1

wave direction

Wavelength is the distance between successive similar points.

S waves are transverse waves, in which the particles move perpendicular to the direction the wave is traveling.

t_2

wave direction

Amplitude is the maximum distance a particle moves from its starting point.

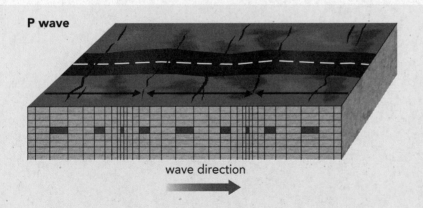

P wave

P waves are longitudinal waves, in which the particles move along the same direction the wave is traveling.

wave direction

Use Models In the art above label the wavelength of the S wave and the P wave on the second and third diagrams.

Mathematical Practices: Model with Mathematics

Mathematical equations can be used to model phenomena that occur in nature. For example, scientists and engineers use equations to model seismic waves, ocean waves, and sound waves.

A sine equation can be used to show the displacement, y, of a particle due to a passing wave with amplitude A and frequency f.

$$y(t) = A \sin(2\pi f t)$$

You can change the parameters A and f in the equation to model any observed data in a time graph.

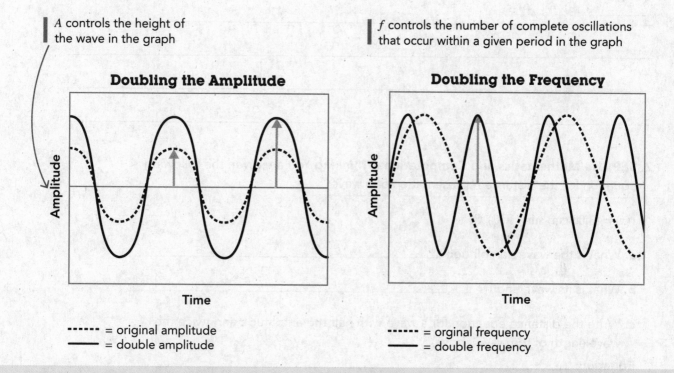

A controls the height of the wave in the graph

Doubling the Amplitude

- - - - - = original amplitude
—— = double amplitude

f controls the number of complete oscillations that occur within a given period in the graph

Doubling the Frequency

- - - - - = orginal frequency
—— = double frequency

Suppose an S wave generated by an earthquake causes a GPS beacon to vary in elevation. You can use mathematics to model the data.

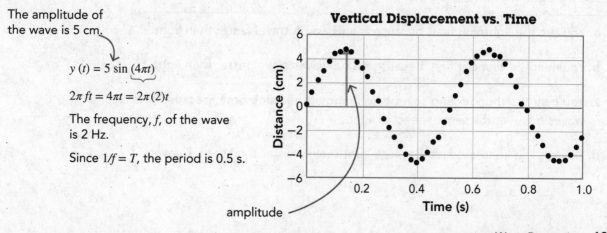

The amplitude of the wave is 5 cm.

$$y(t) = 5 \sin(4\pi t)$$

$$2\pi f t = 4\pi t = 2\pi(2)t$$

The frequency, f, of the wave is 2 Hz.

Since $1/f = T$, the period is 0.5 s.

Vertical Displacement vs. Time

amplitude

3-Dimensional Review

1. DCI Wave Properties The data table below shows the frequencies and wave speeds of two different waves in the same medium. Without performing any calculations, which wave has a shorter wavelength? Explain your answer.

Wave	Frequency (Hz)	Speed (m/s)
A	800 Hz	20 m/s
B	300 Hz	20 m/s

_____

_____

_____

_____

2. SEP Use Mathematics and Computational Thinking You are given the following equation for the distance representation of a wave:

$$y(x) = (3.00 \text{ cm}) \sin [(1.57) \, x]$$

a. What is the wave's amplitude? _____

b. What is its wavelength? _____

c. Write the distance equation for a wave with half the amplitude and twice the wavelength of the wave above.

Equation: _____

3. CCC Cause and Effect A peal of thunder is produced by a bolt of lightning. If you are a mile away from the lightning, do you hear thunder before or after you see the lightning?

a. You see the lightning first, because sound waves travel faster than light.

b. You hear the thunder first, because sound waves travel faster than light.

c. You hear the thunder and see the lightning at the same time, because sound waves travel at the same speed as light.

d. You see the lightning first, because light travels faster than sound waves.

Skills Practice

4. A speaker creates a tone at a frequency of 500.0 Hz. The speaker cone has a maximum displacement of 0.2 cm when turned on. The speed of sound in air is 343 m/s. Construct mathematical and graphical representations of the resulting wave as a function of time.

5. A speaker creates a tone at a frequency of 525 Hz. The speaker cone has a maximum displacement of 0.4 cm when turned on. The speed of sound in air is 343 m/s. Construct mathematical and graphical representations of the resulting wave as a function of time.

6. A speaker creates a tone at a frequency of 261 Hz. The speaker cone has a maximum displacement of 0.6 cm when turned on. The speed of sound in air is 343 m/s. Which equation below is a correct mathematical representation of the resulting wave?

a. $y(t) = 0.6 \sin (1640\ t)$

b. $y(t) = 0.6 \sin (3280\ t)$

c. $y(t) = 0.3 \sin (1640\ t)$

d. $y(t) = 0.3 \sin (3280\ t)$

Wave Behavior and Energy

The characteristics of a wave can change if the location of the wave source changes or if the wave interacts with other waves or itself.

Observed Frequency for a Moving Source of Sound

$$f_o = f_s \left(\frac{v_w}{v_w \pm v_s} \right)$$

where f_o is observed frequency, f_s is source frequency, v_w is wave speed, and v_s is speed of source relative to the observer.

Stationary source:
Both observers hear the frequency that the fire truck produces. ($f_o = f_s$)

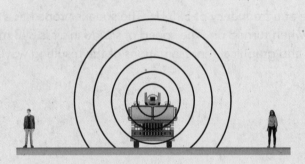

Receding source:
The person on the left hears a lower frequency than the fire truck produces. ($f_o < f_s$)

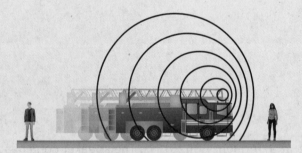

Approaching source:
The person on the right hears a higher frequency than the fire truck produces. ($f_o > f_s$)

Solving problems using the observed frequency formula requires that you choose which mathematical function (+ or –) to use in the denominator of the equation.

Reason Quantitatively In the art above, use a plus sign (+) to label which observer location requires that v_s be added to v_w to find f_o. Use a minus sign (–) to label which observer location requires that v_s be subtracted from v_w to find f_o.

Mathematical Practices: Make Sense of Problems

The reflection of a confined wave results in wave interference and the formation of a standing wave. To solve standing wave problems, link each variable in the frequency formula to components of the system described in the problem, then identify knowns and unknowns. Observe how the variables in the formula for the frequency of a standing wave are linked to the components of the pulley system and the violin.

Frequency of a Standing Wave
$$f = v\frac{1}{\lambda} = \frac{N}{2L}\sqrt{\frac{F_T}{\mu}}$$
where f is frequency, λ is wavelength, v is wave speed, N is an integer (0, 1, 2...), L is the distance between ends, F_T is string tension, and μ is linear density

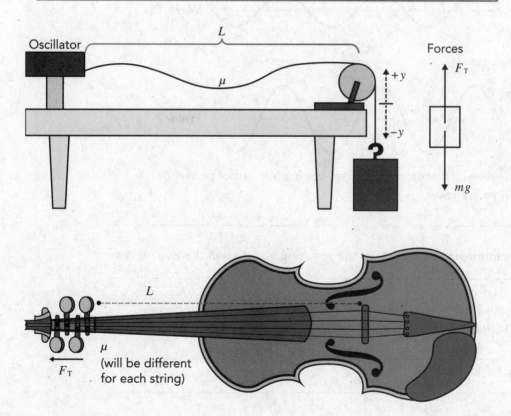

There are two formulas that describe the frequency of a standing wave. Making sense of standing wave problems involves knowing that equivalent portions of the formulas may be substituted for each other.

For example, since v is equivalent to $\sqrt{\frac{F_T}{\mu}}$, then $f = \frac{1}{\lambda}\left(\sqrt{\frac{F_T}{\mu}}\right)$.
Using the same reasoning, the variables that can be substituted for $\frac{1}{\lambda}$ in the equation $f = \frac{1}{\lambda}v$ are $\frac{N}{2L}$.

3-Dimensional Review

1. **DCI Wave Properties** As you stand on the sidewalk, a police car drives toward you with its siren on. As the car passes you, when will the observed frequency be greater, before or after it passes you? As a result, would the perceived wavelength be shorter or longer as the car approaches you?

_____

_____

_____

2. **SEP Use Mathematics and Computational Thinking** The time graph and wave equations for two waves are shown below.

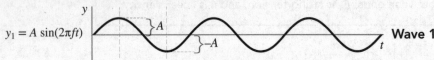

$y_1 = A \sin(2\pi ft)$ **Wave 1**

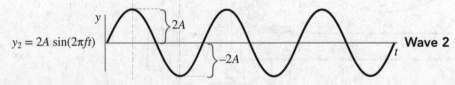

$y_2 = 2A \sin(2\pi ft)$ **Wave 2**

a. Are wave 1 and wave 2 completely in phase, completely out of phase, or neither? Explain your answer.

_____

b. What is the amplitude, in terms of _A_, of the resulting wave when the two waves meet? _____

c. If the second wave had an equation of $y = A \sin(2\pi ft - \pi)$ what would be the amplitude of the resultant wave? Explain your answer using interference.

_____

_____

3. **CCC Cause and Effect** A wave is approaching the beach. As the wave travels from the deep ocean to the shore where it is shallower, which of the following will be a result? Circle all that apply.

a. The wave will have a longer wavelength.

b. The wave will have an unchanged frequency.

c. The wave will have a higher velocity.

d. The wave will have a greater amplitude.

Skills Practice

4. While you are standing still on the sidewalk, an ambulance traveling at 21.0 m/s passes you. The ambulance's siren produces a tone at a frequency of 746 Hz. The speed of sound in air is 343 m/s. What frequency do you hear as the ambulance approaches you? What frequency do you hear as the ambulance moves away from you? According to the Doppler effect, explain why your answer makes sense.

_____

_____

_____

_____

_____

5. While you are standing on the sidewalk, an ambulance traveling at 18.00 m/s passes you. The ambulance's siren produces a tone at a frequency of 848.0 Hz. The speed of the sound in the air is 343.0 m/s. Since the observed frequency of a sound wave can change with a moving source, what is the difference between the frequency you hear as the ambulance approaches you and the frequency you hear as it moves away from you?

a. 895.0 Hz

b. 805.7 Hz

c. 98.36 Hz

d. 89.25 Hz

6. A string attached to a frequency generator passes over a pulley of negligible mass 3.840 m away. A 8.020-kg hanging mass is attached to the other end of the string which has a linear density of $\mu = 0.003800$ kg/m. Determine the speed of a wave on the string. What are the three lowest possible frequencies that the frequency generator must be tuned to in order to produce standing waves? If the string was shorter, would your frequencies get higher or lower? Explain your answer.

_____

_____

_____

Wave Optics

Ray tracing is a process that can be used to determine what type of images form and where they form when light passes through a lens. At least two rays must be drawn to reveal the location of the image. There are three principal rays:

1. A ray parallel to the optical axis, that exits the lens and passes through the focal point
2. A ray straight through the center of the lens (does not bend)
3. A ray going through the focal point that exits the lens parallel to the optical axis

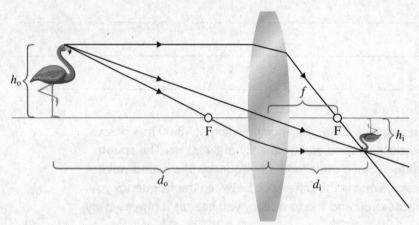

f = focal length
F = focal point
d_o = object distance
d_i = image distance
h_o = object height
h_i = image height

The inverted flamingo is a **real** image. The image location is where the light rays actually converge.

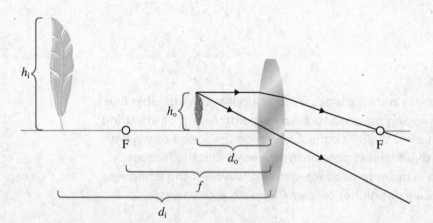

The magnified feather is a **virtual** image. The image location is where light rays appear to converge. To determine the location of the image, the diverging rays must be extended to their apparent point of origin.

Use Models Extend rays in the diagram to show how the location of the feather image was determined. Will you use dotted or solid lines? Why?

_____

_____

Mathematical Practices: Reason Abstractly and Quantitatively

When ray diagrams are drawn to scale, they can be used to help determine the magnification or focal point of a lens.

Magnification Equation (m = magnification)	Lens Equation
$m = \dfrac{h_i}{h_o} = -\dfrac{d_i}{d_o}$	$\dfrac{1}{d_o} + \dfrac{1}{d_i} = \dfrac{1}{f}$

When using these equations, it is important to assign correct mathematical signs (+ and −). Ray tracing diagrams help with this task because they reveal the location of the image. Follow these guidelines:

- Image heights that extend above the principle axis are positive, while those that extend below the axis are negative. Inverted images are negative; upright images are positive.

- Object distances are always assumed to be positive. If the object distance comes out as negative when solving the lens equation, the sign convention is reversed for the object and image distances.

- Image distances are negative when they are on the same side as the object, and positive when they are on the side opposite the object. Real images are positive; virtual images are negative.

Ray tracing diagram and lens formulas can also help you reason about how lenses may be used.

The image distance must be negative (on the same side as the object) in order for a lens to not invert an object.

The ray tracing diagram shown reveals that placing an object within the focal length of a converging lens ($d_o < f$) will result in a magnified, upright image. Also, objects nearer to the focal point of a converging lens produce larger images as $\frac{1}{d_i}$ would decrease nearer to 0. This is why the objective lens of a microscope is positioned just above the prepared microscope slide.

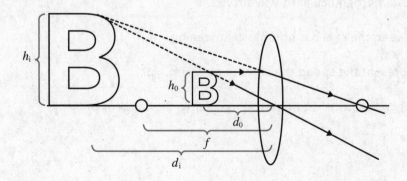

3-Dimensional Review

1. DCI Wave Properties A ray of light hits the surface of water. As it continues into the water, what will happen to the wave speed, wavelength, and direction of the light ray?

_____

_____

_____

_____

2. SEP Engaging in Argument from Evidence Snell's law states that there is a relationship between the velocity and direction of light passing from one medium to another. For a ray of light moving through air into an unknown substance, you are given the following:

$$\frac{\sin(38°)}{v_1} = \frac{\sin(12°)}{v_2}$$

a. Do you expect v_2 to be greater than, less than, or equal to v_1?

_____

b. If the index of the first medium is 1.00, what is the index of refraction of the second medium?

_____

c. Using the definition of the index of refraction, would the speed of light in material 2 be greater than, less than, or equal to the speed of light in a vacuum?

_____

3. CCC Systems and System Models The ray model uses a ray to represent the direction a wave is traveling. Which of the following are true about ray models? Select all that apply.

a. Rays are always drawn perpendicular to wavefronts.

b. The separation between the rays has no physical meaning.

c. Ray models also represent the speed the wave is traveling.

d. For curved wavefronts, the ray is drawn perpendicular to the tangent of the wavefront.

Skills Practice

4. A teacup is placed 0.80 m from a converging lens that has a 0.28-m focal length. Determine whether the image is real or virtual and upright or inverted.

   a. real and inverted

   b. real and upright

   c. virtual and inverted

   d. virtual and upright

5. A baseball is placed 1.40 m from a converging lens that has a 2.20-m focal length. Sketch a ray tracing model to get an appropriate location for the image. Use the lens equation to calculate the location of the image and the magnification. Determine whether the image is real or virtual and upright or inverted. Reflect on your answer by comparing it to your ray tracing model.

6. An image in a book is 1.7 cm tall. You use a magnifying glass with a focal length of 13.0 cm to better view the image. When the magnifying glass is held 7.2 cm from the book, at what height will the letters appear? Sketch a ray tracing model and use the lens equation to determine whether the image is real or virtual and upright or inverted. Reflect on your answer by comparing it to your ray tracing model.

Electromagnetic Waves and Their Properties

The fact that light can be polarized by certain filters, films, or crystals is evidence that light travels in waves that vary in the orientation of their electric fields.

The equation below shows the relationship between the intensity of light incident on a polarizing material or filter (I_0) and the intensity of light leaving the polarizing material or filter (I).

Intensity of Polarized Light
$$I = I_0 \cos^2(\theta)$$
where θ equals the angle between the incident light and the polarizing axis of the filter

Unpolarized light passing through a linear polarizing filter will lose half of its intensity, so $I = 0.5I_0$.

If light passing through a filter is already polarized, the intensity of the light leaving the filter will depend on the angle θ. Here, $\theta = 90°$.

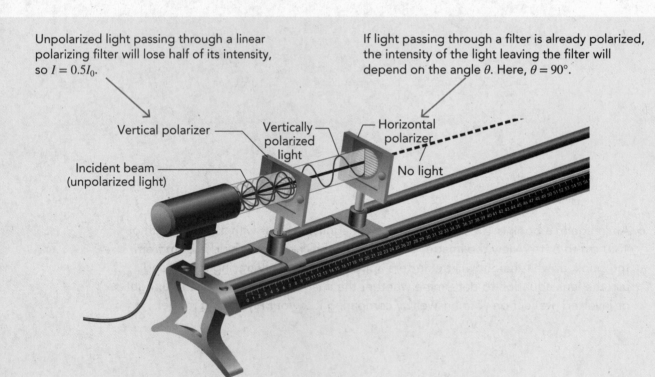

Vertical polarizer

Vertically polarized light

Horizontal polarizer

Incident beam (unpolarized light)

No light

Reason Quantitatively Suppose the horizontal filter is replaced with a 60° polarizing filter. What will be the value of θ? _____

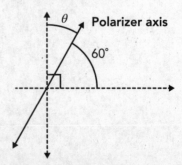

Incident light

θ

Polarizer axis

60°

Mathematical Practices: Reason Abstractly and Quantitatively

When solving polarized light problems, you will need to use what you know about linear polarizing filters and apply the intensity of polarized light equation to each filter in the system sequentially (in order).

Example Suppose unpolarized light passes through a 35° polarizing filter and then a vertical polarizing filter. What percent of the unpolarized light leaves the filter system?

Develop a model
Assign a unique subscript to each light intensity in the filter system

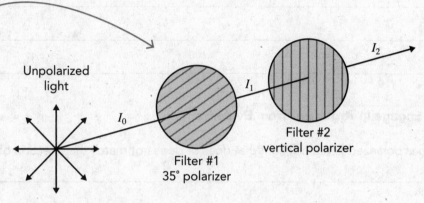

Unpolarized light

I_0

Filter #1
35° polarizer

I_1

Filter #2
vertical polarizer

I_2

Evaluate Filter #1
Apply what you know about linear polarizing filters

The light entering the filter is unpolarized. As it passes through the filter, its intensity decreases by 50%.

$$I_1 = 0.50 I_0$$

Evaluate Filter #2
Apply the intensity of polarized light equation

$$I_2 = I_1 \cos^2(\theta) \quad \{\text{notice the use of subscripts}\}$$

Step 1. Define variables.
I_1 is the light that leaves the first filter, which you found in the previous step.
$I_1 = 0.50 I_0$
θ equals the angle between the polarizer axis and the incident light.
Calculate: $\theta = 90° - 35° = 55°$

Step 2. Enter defined values into the formula and solve.
$I_2 = I_1 \cos^2(\theta)$
$I_2 = (0.50 I_0) \cos^2(55°)$
$I_2 = 0.16 I_0$

Answer: 16% of the original unpolarized light remains.

Repeat Steps 1 and 2 for each new filter added to the system. You can use patterns to find the intensity. For example, if a third filter is added, the intensity of polarized light equation for the third filter is $I_3 = I_2 \cos^2(\theta)$ and $0.16 I_0$ should be substituted for I_2.

3-Dimensional Review

1. DCI Electromagnetic Radiation Electromagnetic radiation can become polarized by reflection or by transmission through certain materials, such as polarizing films. Can this polarization be explained more clearly by the wave model or by the particle model? Why?

_____

_____

_____

_____

2. SEP Engage in Argument from Evidence

a. Does polarized film block light that does or does not match the direction of the film?

_____

_____

b. When you are outside and see a glare from the light, is your glare typically from horizontal or vertical surfaces?

_____

c. For your sunglasses, would you want your polarized film to be horizontal or vertical? Why?

_____

_____

_____

3. CCC Systems and System Models A photodetector has a polarizing film and a source of polarized light. The angle between the incoming light and the polarizer is θ_1. Which answer shows the intensity of the light exiting the polarizer?

a. $I = 0.5I_0$ because light through a polarizer **always** has half the intensity.

b. $I = 0.5I_0$ because light through a polarizer **in this situation** has half the intensity.

c. $I = I_0 \cos^2(\theta_1)$ because light through a polarizer **does not necessarily** have half the intensity in this situation.

d. $I = 0$ because all light is blocked with a polarizer **in this situation**.

Skills Practice

4. Light A and Light B are unpolarized and have intensities noted in the table as shown. If each light is passed through a linear polarizing filter, without performing any calculations, which resulting light will have the higher intensity? Explain your answer.

Light	Intensity
A	1780
B	1260

_____

_____

_____

_____

5. A photodetector has two polarizing films between it and a source of unpolarized light. The first polarizing film is oriented vertically and the second is 60 degrees clockwise from horizontal.

a. What proportion of the original intensity (I_0) passes through after the first filter? Hint: Find I_1.

_____

_____

b. What proportion of the new intensity (I_1) passes through after the second filter?

_____

c. What proportion of the original intensity (I_0) passes through after the second filter?

_____

d. What is the amount of light that passed through the second filter as a percent of I_0? _____

6. A photodetector has three polarizing films between it and a source of unpolarized light. The first polarizing film is oriented vertically, the second is 45 degrees clockwise from the first, and the third is 30 degrees clockwise from the second. Determine the amount of light that reaches the detector as a percent of I_0.

a. 50.00%   **b.** 37.52%

c. 25.00%   **d.** 18.75%

Particle-Wave Duality

Light can act as either a wave or a particle. While the particle nature of light is revealed by specific phenomena, such as the photoelectric effect, scientists rely on the wave nature of light to measure light characteristics.

Light Through a Double-Slit Diffraction Grating

 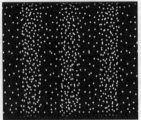 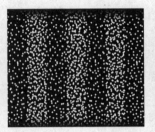 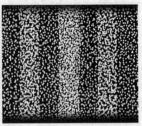

Interpret Data Circle evidence that shows light is a particle. Place a box around evidence that shows light is a wave. Explain your reasoning for each choice.

_____

_____

_____

While the model below shows monochromatic light waves approaching the diffraction grating, light wavelengths are too small to be measured directly. The interference pattern provides measurable quantities that can be used to calculate the wavelength.

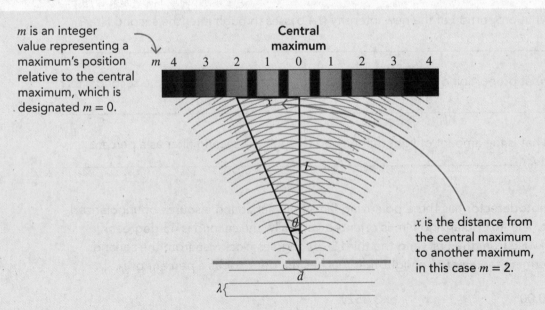

m is an integer value representing a maximum's position relative to the central maximum, which is designated $m = 0$.

Central maximum

x is the distance from the central maximum to another maximum, in this case $m = 2$.

Use Models Draw a triangle to the right of the central maximum that you can use to find θ when $m = 3$.

Mathematical Practices: Make Use of Structure

Double-slit interference problems have a consistent structure because the $d \ll L$ condition tends to be satisfied by the construction of most experimental set-ups, and they can require the use of two formulas:

> ### Double-Slit Interference Patterns
>
> when $d \ll L$
>
> $d \sin(\theta) = m\lambda$ and $x = \frac{m\lambda L}{d}$
>
> d = distance between the slits
> θ = angle between L and the maximum
> λ = wavelength of incident light
> x = distance on the screen, left or right from the center
> L = distance between the screen and the slits
> m = integer indicating the position of the maximum
>   relative to the central maximum

You can make use of this structure to apply a consistent solution strategy for double-slit interference problems:

1. Draw a picture

2. List knowns and unknowns and assign variables

3. Convert all distance units to meters

4. Begin with the formula that includes only one unknown

5. Solve and evaluate the answer

Sample problem: Scientists set up a diffraction grating so that it is 2.2 m away from a screen. The slits in the grating are 0.05 mm apart. As the light from a synthetic-diamond laser shines through the grating, the scientists measure the angle to the third maximum to find $\theta = 12°$.

What is the wavelength of the laser light? What is the distance (x) to the third maximum?

The distances need to be converted to the same units. Check your conversion ratios to make sure you apply them correctly.

You will need to choose the double-slit interference formula in which λ (wavelength) is the only unknown.

Solution: The formula that includes only one unknown is $d \sin(\theta) = m\lambda$. After converting the value of d into meters, solving this equation for the wavelength (λ) provides the value needed to find x using the second equation, $x = \frac{m\lambda L}{d}$. ($\lambda = 3.5 \times 10^{-6}$ m; $x = 0.46$ m)

3-Dimensional Review

1. DCI Wave Properties Which of the following phenomena best supports the particle theory of light? Explain your answer.

Reflection   Polarization   Photoelectric Effect

_____

_____

_____

_____

_____

2. SEP Engage in Argument from Evidence You are given the following equation for the double-slit interference pattern of a light ($d\sin\theta = m\lambda$).

$$2.32 \times 10^{-4} \sin(4.58°) = m(3.33 \times 10^{-7})$$

a. Based on the angle you are given above, about how far should the distance be to the farthest maximum? Hint: give your answer in terms of L.

_____

_____

b. If you were to decrease the distance between the slits, how would that impact the angle to the same maximum and the resulting image?

_____

c. What would be the equation for the distance on the screen between the L-line and the farthest maximum within the 4.58°? Hint: Give your answer in terms of m. _____

3. CCC Systems and System Models A double-slit apparatus records an interference pattern being built up gradually by the detection of individual photons. **Immediately** after you start collecting data, which hypothesis will your data support?

a. Light behaves as a particle because of the diffraction pattern seen.

b. Light behaves as a particle because each individual photon strikes the screen at one point.

c. Light behaves as a wave because of the diffraction pattern seen.

d. Light behaves as a wave because each individual photon strikes the screen at one point.

Skills Practice

4. A laser beam with a wavelength of 348 nm is directed through two slits that are 241 cm from a screen. The distance between the two slits is 0.0800 mm. The angle is 3.14 degrees and the distance on the screen between the *L*-line and the farthest maximum is denoted *x*. Sketch a general picture of this situation and list all known and unknown variables with SI units.

5. A laser beam with a wavelength of 4.12×10^{-7} m is directed through two slits that are 1.02 m from a screen. The distance between the two slits is 3.10×10^{-4} m. For an angle of 2.02°, what is the distance on the screen between the *L*-line and the farthest maximum within the 2.02°? Justify your answer.

6. A laser is projected through a double slit in a barrier that is 3.58 m from a projection screen. The two slits are 1.89×10^{-4} m apart from each other. If the 98th maximum is 0.89 m from the central maximum, what is likely the color of the laser's light?

a. orange

b. yellow

c. green

d. blue

Electromagnetic Radiation and Matter

When light photons strike matter, they can excite or eject bound electrons. Evidence for these photon-electron interactions and the energy transfers they cause include absorption and emission spectra, the glow of fluorescent lights, and the damaging effects of ionizing radiation on living tissue and DNA.

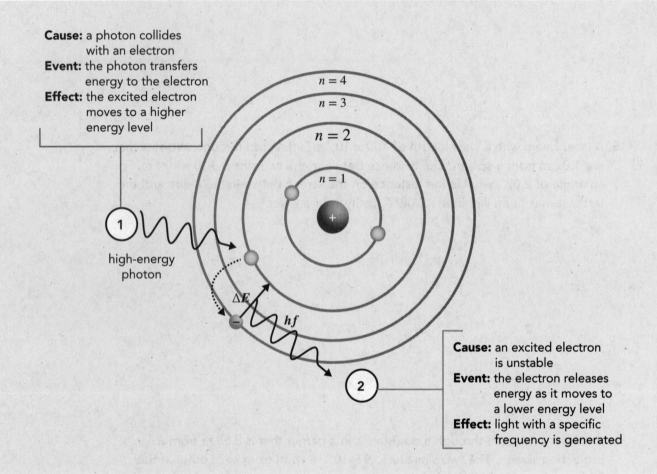

Cause: a photon collides with an electron
Event: the photon transfers energy to the electron
Effect: the excited electron moves to a higher energy level

high-energy photon

1

$n = 4$
$n = 3$
$n = 2$
$n = 1$

ΔE

hf

2

Cause: an excited electron is unstable
Event: the electron releases energy as it moves to a lower energy level
Effect: light with a specific frequency is generated

Support Your Explanation with Evidence A scientist observes multiple light frequencies emitted from a gas excited by photon bombardment. Explain how this is possible using evidence from the diagram.

_____

_____

_____

Science Practices: Construct Explanations

Explanations typically describe cause-and-effect relationships. Sometimes, multiple cause-and-effect relationships must be combined together to provide a complete explanation.

Consider the cause-and-effect relationships that can be combined together to provide a complete explanation of how sunscreen protects skin from harmful UV rays.

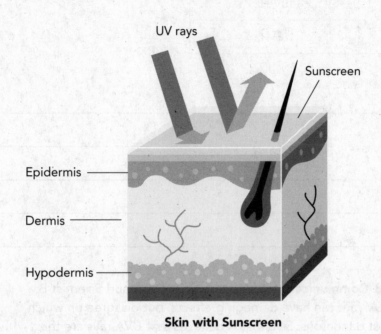

Skin with Sunscreen

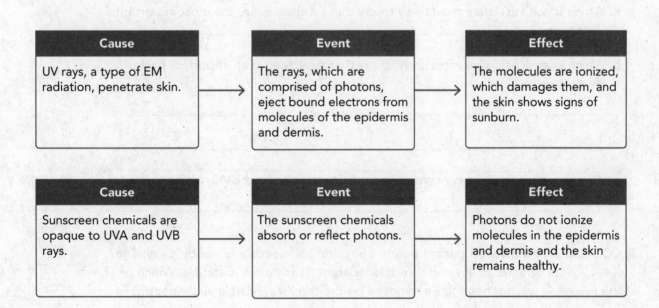

Cause		Event		Effect
UV rays, a type of EM radiation, penetrate skin.	→	The rays, which are comprised of photons, eject bound electrons from molecules of the epidermis and dermis.	→	The molecules are ionized, which damages them, and the skin shows signs of sunburn.

Cause		Event		Effect
Sunscreen chemicals are opaque to UVA and UVB rays.	→	The sunscreen chemicals absorb or reflect photons.	→	Photons do not ionize molecules in the epidermis and dermis and the skin remains healthy.

3-Dimensional Review

1. **DCI Electromagnetic Radiation** The frequencies of two electromagnetic waves are given below. How do these frequencies relate to wavelength, and what would be the likely results of long-term exposure to each of the two EM waves? Confirm your thoughts by determining what type of waves they are and their resulting energies.

Wave	Frequency
1	10^{11} Hz
2	10^{23} Hz

_____

_____

_____

_____

_____

2. **SEP Obtain, Evaluate, & Communicate Information** Scientist A and Scientist B agree that exposure to UV rays can have damaging effects, but disagree on which form of UV ray is the most dangerous. Scientist A believes that UVA rays are the most damaging, and Scientist B believes that UVB rays are the most damaging.

   a. Which scientist(s) is/are most likely to say that sunglasses are the most important UV defense? _____

   b. Which scientist(s) is/are most likely to say that sunscreen is an important part of UV protection?

   _____

   _____

   c. Why is neither scientist concerned about protection against UVC rays?

   _____

3. **CCC Cause and Effect** A patient enters a hospital and needs a full body X-ray. The X-ray will be opaque to any metal and transparent to any cloth materials. Which of the following will not need to be removed before the X-ray? Circle all that apply.

   a. a necklace with a metal chain   **b.** a cotton shirt

   c. steel-toed boots   **d.** a pair of socks

Skills Practice

4. UVA and UVB rays are damaging. UVA rays penetrate the epidermis and disperse in the dermis. UVB rays simply penetrate the epidermis. How do sunscreens protect us from UV rays and what happens to the UV energy? Are broad-spectrum sunscreens opaque to UVA and UVB rays? Explain your reasoning.

_____

_____

_____

5. Are polarized sunglasses and UV-blocking sunglasses the same? Construct an explanation for how they are the same or different.

_____

_____

_____

_____

6. When asked how sunscreen should be used to block skin damage from the most damaging UV rays, your friend gives the following answer:

Sunscreen should be used to block all UV rays, especially UVC rays. UVC rays are the highest energy so they can potentially cause the most damage. High-energy radiation is the most dangerous because it can cause DNA damage and cell death.

Construct an explanation for which part of your friend's answer is correct and which part is incorrect. Explain your reasoning.

_____

_____

_____

_____

Digital Information

Binary code uses a series of 1s and 0s to represent information. It is ideal for computing because 1s and 0s can correspond to the presence or absence of charge running through computer circuitry and to north and south magnetic orientations in hard drive storage systems. It is also a versatile code. Patterns of 1s and 0s can represent characters (letters, symbols, numbers) and they can communicate yes/no commands, such as "yes—energize this segment of a digital display."

Digital Displays and Binary Code

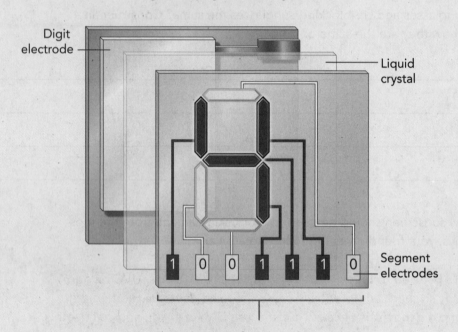

Digit electrode

Liquid crystal

1 0 0 1 1 1 0

Segment electrodes

The sequence of zeros and ones along the bottom of this image indicate which segments of the display should be energized by the electrodes.

Identify Patterns In the system presented in the diagram, what pattern of 0s and 1s will cause the digital display to show the number five (5)? _____

Mathematical Practices: Use Tools Strategically

Since binary code can be used in different ways, rules must be established for how it will be used in each specific case. Tables can be used strategically to define rules for binary code. In general, tables are useful tools because they help organize information. Depending on how information is entered into rows and columns, tables can help you sort items into categories, display a sequence, perform repeated calculations, or analyze patterns in data.

Look at the table below, then read about how each row is helpful in converting the number 26 to binary code.

Place value	2^4	2^3	2^2	2^1	2^0
Subtraction steps	$26 - 16 = 10 \longrightarrow$	$10 - 8 = 2 \longrightarrow$		$\longrightarrow 2 - 2 = 0$	
Binary code	1	1	0	1	0

Place value
The place value row shows how many power of 2 values are needed to represent the number. The highest power of 2 in the row must be the closest power of two to the number you want to convert, without being greater than that number. In the example above, $2^5 = 32$ which is greater than 26, so 2^4 must be the first column in the table. Then you add a column for each lower power of 2 until you reach 2^0. This means the code for 26 will require 5 binary code values.

Subtraction steps
In the next row, subtract the largest power of 2 possible from the number you want to convert as long as the result is 0 or greater. Skip any calculation that would result in a negative number. For example, you omit the calculation for 2^2 because the subtraction step would be: $2 - 4 = -2$.

Binary code
Add 1s and 0s to this row to write the binary code. Add a "1" for powers of 2 that can be subtracted without resulting in a negative number. Add a "0" for other powers of 2.

Check your answer
You can check your answer by working the calculation the other way, from binary to decimal. The binary number 11010 means to add the following decimal numbers:

$$16 + 8 + 0 + 2 + 0 = 26$$

3-Dimensional Review

1. DCI Wave Properties When digitizing a sound, what wave property is captured in sampling? How does this create a sound wave?

_____

_____

_____

2. SEP Asking Questions and Defining Problems
Binary code uses 1s and 0s to represent information.

a. What question regarding charge might computers need to answer? How can binary help answer this question?

_____

_____

_____

b. How can binary code solve the problem of representing a character from the alphabet using a digital display?

_____

_____

_____

c. What problems might cause us to not use binary code in our day-to-day life?

_____

_____

3. CCC Stability and Change Which of the following technologies has contributed to the stability of digital media?

a. a computer network server

b. a cassette tape

c. a video game

d. an MP3 video

Skills Practice

4. Convert the number 182 from decimal (base 10) to binary (base 2). Fill in the tables below to assist you with your conversion.

Decimal Place Value		
10^2 (hundreds)	10^1 (tens)	10^0 (ones)

Binary Place Value							
2^7	2^6	2^5	2^4	2^3	2^2	2^1	2^0

5. Convert the number 478 from decimal (base 10) to binary (base 2).

6. The following number is given in binary (base 2): 101111. What is this answer in decimal format (base 10)?

a. 26

b. 47

c. 94

d. 82

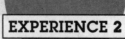
Capturing and Transmitting Information

Technologies that capture or transmit information take advantage of how waves transfer energy and how they can interact with matter. Each technology includes a way for waves to interact with a target substance and through this interaction a way to capture or transmit wave energy by converting it into a new form. Some of these technologies include digital cameras as well as medical imaging devices such as ultrasound and MRI machines. Sound is commonly captured and transmitted using microphones.

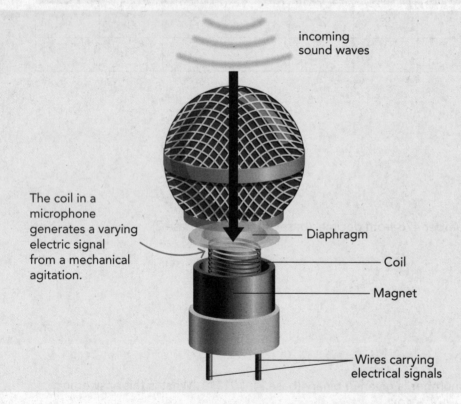

incoming sound waves

The coil in a microphone generates a varying electric signal from a mechanical agitation.

Diaphragm

Coil

Magnet

Wires carrying electrical signals

To design a microphone or other technology, engineers define a problem they would like to solve and then they ask questions about how they can use scientific understanding and materials to solve the problem. Here are some questions that engineers might ask to design a microphone.

- How can sound waves be converted into electrical signals?

- Can we use sound waves to move the coil of an electromagnet so that it generates an electrical signal?

- What characteristics will the diaphragm material need to have?

Evaluate Technical Information Study the diagram about how a microphone works. Circle evidence in the diagram or its text that shows that waves interact with matter. Place a box around evidence in the diagram or its text that shows wave energy converted into a new form.

Science Practices: Asking Questions

Asking questions also helps engineers to understand the suitability of a design. When testing or optimizing a design, engineers ask questions to help them analyze the structure and function of different parts of the device, as well as how the device meets design criteria overall.

In the same way, you can **ask questions** about a technology or technology model to help you analyze how a design meets criteria or to help you interpret how a model represents the structure and function of a design.

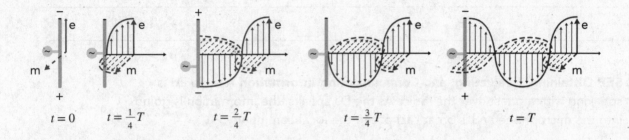

Question	Answer
What does the model represent?	how an antenna transmits a signal
What represents the antenna in the diagram?	the vertical bar
What do the symbols represent?	~ = a changing electric signal; + and − = charge on the antenna; parallel arrows (e) = electric field; perpendicular arrows (m) = magnetic field
Why is time given in terms of T, the period of a wave?	to link time to the electromagnetic wave pattern in the diagram
What happens on the antenna as time passes?	The charge separation reverses direction. First, negative charge is marked at the top of the antenna, then positive charge, then negative charge.
What happens to the electric and magnetic fields as time passes?	They oscillate back and forth to form a sinusoidal pattern.
What causes each field to change?	The changing electric signal causes the changing electric field. The changing electric field causes the changing magnetic field.

3-Dimensional Review

1. **DCI Information Technologies and Instrumentation** Microphones convert sound into electrical signals. Digital photography, on the other hand, converts light into information. How does digital photography use red, green, and blue light filters to create a photograph?

_____

_____

_____

_____

2. **SEP Obtaining, Evaluating, and Communicating Information** A radio DJ is speaking with a guest over the radio. As the DJ speaks, the information is going into the microphone and is broadcast out to the local community.

   a. How is the microphone transducing between the wave energy of sound and electrical energy?

   _____

   _____

   _____

   b. How is the DJ's radio antenna broadcasting the story to the community?

   _____

   _____

   _____

   c. If the DJ is broadcasting live, will there be a delay between when the DJ speaks and when the listeners hear the story?

   _____

   _____

   _____

3. **CCC Cause and Effect** Which of the following would **NOT** be a cause for a medical professional to use ultrasound technology?

   a. capturing an image that will take several minutes of exposure

   b. imaging internal organs for diagnosis of swelling

   c. tattoo removal

   d. assessing a heart valve problem

Skills Practice

4. Ask a question about microphone efficiency. Then answer the question.

_____

_____

_____

_____

5. Ask a question about how MRIs work to align the atoms in a body and whether it is a temporary or permanent alignment. Then answer the question.

_____

_____

_____

_____

_____

_____

6. A teacher receives the following answer from a student: "The electric and magnetic fields in the wave induce a current in the wires. As the field alternates, the current alternates and the original signal is reproduced." Which of the following was likely the question the student was asked to produce this answer?

a. How does an antenna transmit information?

b. How does an antenna receive information?

c. How does a CT scan produce an image?

d. How does a speaker produce sound?

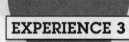

Capturing and Transmitting Energy

All technologies depend on efficient energy transformation. Wireless chargers, microwave ovens, and radiotherapy devices transform electrical energy into energy in EM waves, while solar panels transform solar energy into electrical energy. These energy transformations are not perfect. Electrical components become warm, converting some useful energy into waste heat. A percentage of EM waves incident upon a solar panel simply reflect back into the atmosphere.

Scientists and engineers evaluate the efficiency of energy-dependent devices by comparing total energy input with useful energy output.

Efficiency of Energy Transformation
$$Eff = \frac{E_{out}}{E_{in}} \times 100$$
Eff = efficiency, expressed as a percent
E_{out} = useful energy output
E_{in} = total energy input

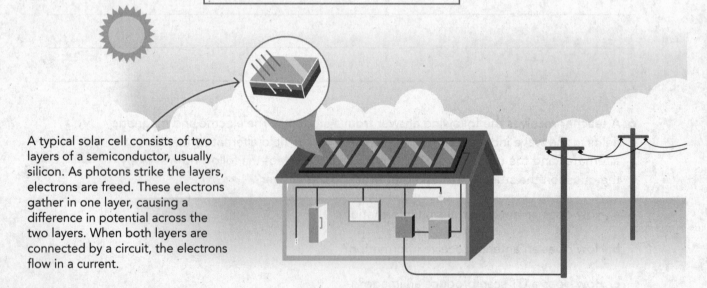

A typical solar cell consists of two layers of a semiconductor, usually silicon. As photons strike the layers, electrons are freed. These electrons gather in one layer, causing a difference in potential across the two layers. When both layers are connected by a circuit, the electrons flow in a current.

Construct an Argument Would adding more solar panels to the house increase the efficiency of the solar cell system? Use the efficiency equation in your reasoning.

_____

_____

_____

_____

Mathematical Practices: Make Sense of Problems

Mathematically proficient students start by explaining to themselves the meaning of a problem and looking for entry points to its solution. They analyze goals, givens, and relationships—which are often expressed as equations or revealed by units.

Consider the efficiency problem below, then review the questions someone solving the problem might ask to make sense of the problem and to develop a solution.

Problem:

A home solar energy system produces 25.5 kWh each day (8 hours) using a 20 m^2 solar panel system labeled with an 18% efficiency rating. If 1000 W/m^2 of solar energy (power per unit area) reaches the Earth's surface each hour during the day, is the solar system performing as well as advertised?

Making sense of the problem:

*What is the **goal** of the problem?*
- To compare the actual efficiency with the advertised efficiency

What will I need to calculate?
- The actual efficiency

*What information is **given**?*
- Energy produced each day in KWh = energy out (E_{out}) = 25.5 kWh
- Energy power provided by the sun over area = 1000 W/m^2 for 8 hours
- Area of the solar cell system = 20 m^2

*How can **relationships** (equations and units) help me develop a solution?*

$$Eff = \frac{E_{out}}{E_{in}} \times 100$$

- To find the actual efficiency, E_{out} and E_{in} need to be in the same units. E_{out} is given in kWh. Use other givens to find E_{in} in KWh.

- The power per unit area from the sun is in W/m^2, so convert watts to kilowatts, then multiply by the area of the solar cell system and the number of hours the system is used:

$$E_{in} = 1000 \text{ W/m}^2 \times 1 \text{ kW/1000 W} \times 20 \text{ m}^2 \times 8 \text{ h} = 160 \text{ kWh}$$

$$\text{Actual } Eff = \frac{25.5 \text{ kWh}}{160 \text{ kWh}} \times 100 = 16 \text{ %}$$

The actual efficiency is 2% less than the advertised efficiency.

Does my solution make sense?
- Yes, the actual efficiency is a reasonable value

3-Dimensional Review

1. DCI Information Technologies and Instrumentation How do solar panels convert the sun's energy into electricity?

_____

_____

_____

_____

2. SEP Obtaining, Evaluating, and Communicating Information While preparing dinner a family decided to bake chicken inside their convection oven, heat up green beans on their stove-top, and microwave left-over potatoes.

a. How does the convection oven cook the chicken?

_____

_____

_____

b. How does the stove heat the green beans?

_____

_____

c. How does the microwave warm the potatoes?

_____

_____

_____

_____

3. CCC Cause and Effect Solar panels consist of solar cells which convert solar energy to electrical energy. If a building is powered by solar panels, which of the following would cause an increased efficiency in the solar power of a building?

a. adding a back-up battery generator to the building

b. increasing the number of solar cells per solar panel

c. increasing the number of solar panels per building

d. decreasing the amount of light refracted away from each solar panel

Skills Practice

4. Wireless chargers work through an alternating current in the charger that induces a current in the secondary coil inside the phone. The newest wireless charger boasts a 87% efficiency rating. If the phone requires 8.90 kilowatts of energy to reach a full charge, how many kilowatts of energy need to be supplied to the charger for the phone to fully charge?

5. A family buys a new brand of solar panel with a 34% efficiency rating. Their home uses about 26.5 kilowatt-hours of energy per day. Assuming nine hours of useful energy collection in a day, how much area would an array of solar panels have to cover to power their home? Assume 1,000 W/m^2 of solar energy (power per unit area) reaches the Earth's surface.

6. Radiotherapy is the medical use of electromagnetic radiation to treat illnesses such as cancer. A hospital buys a new linear accelerator to perform their radiosurgery. This machine requires 28.4 kilowatts of energy to emit 18.6 kilowatts of power. What is the efficiency rating of the machine as a percent?

a. 0.650%

b. 1.69%

c. 65.4%

d. 89.8%

Nuclear Particles

The Standard Model of particle physics identifies three classes of elementary particles: quarks, leptons, and bosons.

Classifying Elementary Particles

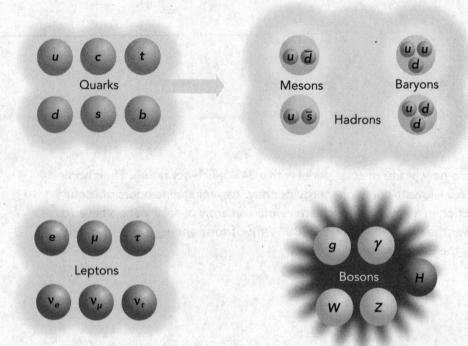

Quarks are observed to combine in groups of two or three to form "heavy" particles known as hadrons. Groups of two quarks are referred to as mesons and groups of three quarks are called baryons. Leptons, including electrons and neutrinos, are "light" particles which do not form combinations. Bosons are particles which carry the fundamental forces that allow quarks and leptons to interact. Examples of bosons would include the gluons that carry the strong force and photons such as gamma rays which carry the electromagnetic force.

Using Models The sub-atomic particles most important to your everyday experience are protons, neutrons, electrons, and photons. Identify how each of these particles should be classified according to the Standard Model. If any of these particles are hadrons, describe the composition of these particles in terms of quarks.

_____

_____

_____

_____

Mathematical Practices: Model with Mathematics

Although the exact size and shape of a nucleus are difficult to describe, the nucleus can be modeled as a sphere of uniform density. The volume of the nucleus can be assumed to be proportional to the mass number, A, which is the total number of protons and neutrons. Since the formula for volume of a sphere is $V = \frac{4}{3}\pi R^3$, this means that the radius (R) should be proportional to $A^{1/3}$ (the cube root of A). The specific formula for the radius of a nucleus is given below:

$$R \approx (1.2 \times 10^{-15} \text{ m})A^{1/3}$$

You can use this equation to estimate the radius of a nucleus if you know the mass number. For example, the only stable isotope of gold has a mass number of 197 since the nucleus consists of 79 protons and 118 neutrons. To calculate the radius of the nucleus of this atom (^{197}Au), you can set $A = 197$ in the preceding equation:

$$R \approx (1.2 \times 10^{-15} \text{ m})(197)^{1/3}$$

$$R \approx 7.0 \times 10^{-15} \text{ m}$$

The radius of a gold atom is reported to be 166 pm or 1.66×10^{-10} m, which is larger than the nucleus by a factor of more than twenty thousand. This is consistent with the results of the Geiger-Marsden gold foil experiment which showed that most of the volume of a gold atom is actually empty space.

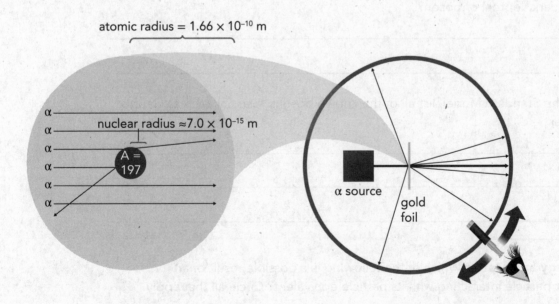

3-Dimensional Review

1. DCI Nuclear Processes In your own words, explain how a gamma ray interacting with a nucleus of another gamma ray can create mass out of energy.

_____

_____

_____

2. SEP Developing and Using Models

a. What are the three categories that the Standard Model organizes particles into? How are they differentiated?

_____

_____

_____

_____

b. Using the Standard Model, determine the mass and charge of a muon neutrino. Is it a quark, lepton, or boson?

_____

_____

c. Using the Standard Model, list all of the known bosons. Classify each as Gauge or Scalar.

_____

_____

_____

3. CCC Energy and Matter Which of the following is a possible result of an antimatter particle interacting with its particle equivalent? Circle all that apply.

a. positron and electron annihilation

b. 2 massless gamma ray photons

c. 1.022 MeV of energy

d. an electron/positron pair

Skills Practice

4. Calculate how much greater the nuclear radius of the only stable isotope of aluminum, $^{27}_{13}\text{Al}$, is than the only stable isotope of sodium, $^{23}_{11}\text{Na}$.

5. Calculate how much greater the nuclear radius of the largest stable isotope of lead, $^{208}_{82}\text{Pb}$, is than the smallest stable isotope of silicon, $^{28}_{14}\text{Si}$.

6. Calculate how much denser an atomic nucleus is than a piece of quartz (2320 kg/m³).

a. 1.0×10^{-14}

b. 9.9×10^{13}

c. 1.0×10^{14}

d. 5.3×10^{20}

Nuclear Forces

The protons and neutrons in an atomic nucleus are attracted to each other by the strong force. Although this force primarily affects the quarks within a single proton or neutron, it also results in an attraction between nucleons that dominates any effect of the other fundamental forces (weak force, electromagnetic force, and gravity). The existence of this attraction means that an input of energy would be required in order to break the nucleus up into separate particles. The amount of energy that would be required for this process is referred to as the binding energy since this is also the amount of energy that would be released when the particles bind together to form a nucleus.

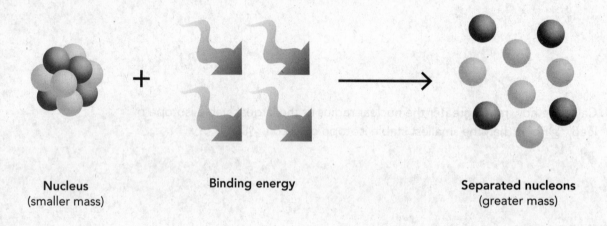

Nucleus
(smaller mass)

Binding energy

Separated nucleons
(greater mass)

Einstein's mass-energy relationship, $E = mc^2$, implies that if you are adding energy to the system when you separate the nuclear particles, the system must have more mass at the end of the process.

Engaging in Argument from Evidence Based on the information presented above, explain in terms of mass and energy what you expect to happen when a nucleus is formed from separated particles.

_____

_____

Mathematical Practices: Attend to Precision

If the mass of a nucleus is known, you can calculate the binding energy by comparing its mass to the mass of the separated particles using the equation below.

Binding Energy of a Nucleus
$$B = (Zm_p + Nm_n - m_{nucleus})c^2$$

B = binding energy

Z = number of protons

$m_{nucleus}$ = mass of the nucleus

N = number of neutrons

m_n = mass of a neutron (939.57 MeV/c^2)

m_p = mass of a proton (938.27 MeV/c^2)

c = speed of light

Since the value of c^2 is extremely large, even the large amounts of energy involved in nuclear processes correspond to changes in mass that are a tiny fraction of the total mass of the particles involved. Thus, it is important that you keep more significant figures than usual in your calculations since you are calculating a small difference between the mass of the reactants and the mass of the products.

For example, a ^{12}C nucleus with six protons and six neutrons has a mass of 12.0000 u, and since 1 u = 931.494 MeV/c^2, you can express the mass of this nucleus as 11,177.9 MeV/c^2. Using this value along with the proton and neutron masses given above, you can calculate the binding energy for the ^{12}C nucleus:

$$B = \left[(6 \text{ protons})\left(938.27 \, \tfrac{\text{MeV}}{c^2}\right) + (6 \text{ neutrons})\left(939.57 \, \tfrac{\text{MeV}}{c^2}\right) - \left(11{,}177.9 \, \tfrac{\text{MeV}}{c^2}\right)\right]c^2$$

$$B = (5629.62 + 5637.42 - 11{,}177.9)\text{MeV}$$

$$B = (11{,}267.04 - 11{,}177.9)\text{MeV} = 89.1 \text{ MeV}$$

The difference between the energy equivalent of the separate particles and the energy equivalent of the total mass of the nucleus is only $\left(\frac{89.1}{11{,}177.9}\right) \times 100 \approx 0.8\%$, so waiting to round off until the end of the calculation is important to getting a precise answer.

3-Dimensional Review

1. DCI Nuclear Processes What happens during beta-plus decay? What happens to the total number of particles in the nucleus?

_____

_____

_____

2. SEP Developing and Using Models

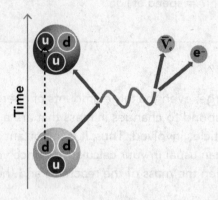

a. What type of decay is in the model? Explain your answer.

_____

_____

b. Will this result in a release or absorption of energy?

_____

c. What is the role of the W boson in this decay?

_____

3. CCC Energy and Matter According to Einstein's mass-energy relationship, which of the following could result in more mass at the end of a nuclear process?

a. the joining of two bottom quarks

b. an unstable nucleus undergoing beta-minus decay

c. the interaction of a positron and an electron

d. the interaction of two gamma rays

Skills Practice

4. What is the average binding energy per nucleon in the ^{208}Pb nucleus if the mass of its nucleus is 193,752 MeV/c^2?

5. What is the average binding energy per nucleon in the ^{23}Na nucleus if the mass of its nucleus is 21,425 MeV/c^2?

6. What is the average binding energy per nucleon in the ^{27}Al nucleus if the mass of its nucleus is 25,151 MeV/c^2?

a. 2.9 MeV per nucleon

b. 7.4 MeV per nucleon

c. 18 MeV per nucleon

d. 20 MeV per nucleon

Fission and Fusion

Fission and fusion are two important types of nuclear reactions. Nuclear fission refers to a process in which a large nucleus is split into two smaller nuclei, while nuclear fusion refers to a process in which two small nuclei are combined to form a larger nucleus.

Whether or not a given nuclear reaction will release energy depends on the relative positions of the reactant and product nuclei on the curve of nuclear binding energy shown below. Since binding energy is the energy released when a nucleus is formed, energy will be released in a nuclear reaction if the average binding energy in the products is greater than the average binding energy in the reactants.

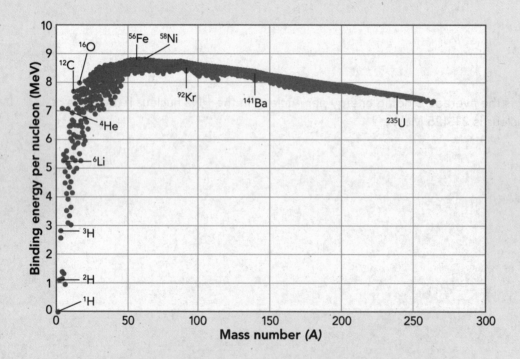

Analyzing and Interpreting Data Draw a vertical line where the curve changes from upward sloping to downward sloping to divide the chart above into two regions. For each region explain whether nuclei in that region will be more likely to release energy by undergoing fission or fusion.

_____

_____

_____

Mathematical Practices: Use Appropriate Tools Strategically

Nuclear reactions can convert very small amounts of mass into large amounts of energy. The most obvious way to calculate the energy released by a particular nuclear reaction would be to calculate the difference in mass between the reactants and products and then use that mass in the equation $E = mc^2$ to calculate the corresponding amount of energy.

However, since mass and energy are equivalent, you can also calculate the energy released using the average binding energy of the reactants and products, since the total number of nuclear particles or baryons has to remain constant. Multiplying the average binding energy by the number of nucleons gives the total binding energy for a given nucleus, and the difference between the total binding energy in the reactants and the products will be the energy released in the reaction.

The isotope of the synthetic element plutonium used most commonly in fission reactions is ^{239}Pu with an average binding energy of 7.56 MeV/nucleon. Typical products from fission of this isotope might be the isotopes ^{134}Xe and ^{103}Zr (plus free neutrons).

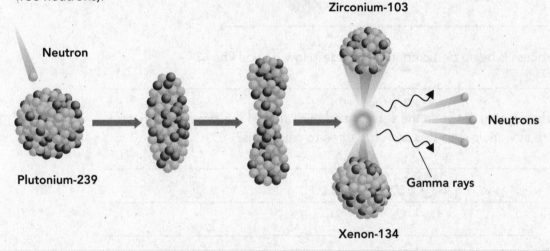

Zirconium-103

Neutron

Plutonium-239

Neutrons

Gamma rays

Xenon-134

Even without being given exact values, you can use information available in the binding energy chart to estimate that a ^{134}Xe nuclide with a mass number of 134 might have an average binding energy ≈ 8.25 MeV/nucleon and that a ^{103}Zr nuclide with a mass number of 103 should have a slightly greater average binding energy ≈ 8.35 MeV/nucleon.

Since the total binding energy is expected to be greater for the products, you should calculate that first and then subtract the binding energy for the reactant:

ΔE = (product binding energy) − (reactant binding energy)

= [(134 nucleons)(8.25 MeV/nucleon) + (103 nucleons)

(8.35 MeV/nucleon)] − (239 nucleons)(7.56 MeV/nucleon)

= [1105.50 MeV + 860.05 MeV] − 1806.84 MeV

= 1965.55 MeV − 1806.84 MeV = 158.71 MeV $\approx$ 159 MeV

3-Dimensional Review

1. DCI Nuclear Processes In your own words, describe the processes of fission and fusion. What happens to the total number of protons and neutrons in each process?

_____

_____

_____

2. SEP Developing and Using Models

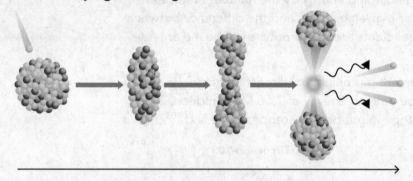

a. What process is being depicted in the image? How do you know?

_____

b. What is happening between the second and third step of this process? What forces are at work in step two and step three to cause this?

_____

_____

_____

_____

c. In the final stage, what happens to most of the energy?

_____

_____

3. CCC Energy and Matter Which of the following is conserved in any nuclear process? Circle all that apply.

a. mass

b. number of neutrons

c. number of nucleons

d. number of protons

Skills Practice

4. How much more energy is released per gram by the fission of ^{235}U into ^{208}Pb and ^{23}Na than the combustion of methane (50.1 kJ/g) if the binding energies of the reactants and products of the nuclear reaction are 7.59 MeV, 7.87 MeV, and 8.21 MeV, respectively? Express your answer in scientific notation.

5. How much more energy is released per gram by the fission of ^{235}U into ^{144}Cs and ^{90}Rb than the combustion of methane (50.1 kJ/g) if the binding energies of the reactants and products of the nuclear reaction are 7.59 MeV, 8.21 MeV, and 8.63 MeV, respectively?

6. How much more energy is released per gram by the fission of ^{235}U into ^{90}Rb and ^{142}Xe than the combustion of methane (50.1 kJ/g) if the binding energies of the reactants and products of the nuclear reaction are 7.59 MeV, 8.63 MeV, and 8.23 MeV, respectively?

a. 0.131 million

b. 1.31 million

c. 13.1 million

d. 131 million

Radioactive Decay

While a large sample of a radioactive element will decay at a predictable rate, each decay is a random event. This means that some of the atoms in the sample will take a very long time to decay compared to others. As a result, the curve representing the decay of a radioactive sample has a very long "tail" and the mean life is longer than the half-life. Half-lives, $t_{1/2}$, and mean lives, τ, are related by this equation:

$$t_{1/2} = \tau \ln(2) = 0.693\tau$$

Either the mean life or half-life may be used in equations for exponential decay.

Mean Lives and Half-Lives
$N = N_0 e^{-\frac{t}{\tau}}$ and $N = N_0 e^{-\frac{0.693t}{t_{1/2}}}$
N = number of remaining atoms $\quad \tau$ = mean life
N_0 = initial number of atoms $\quad t_{1/2}$ = half-life

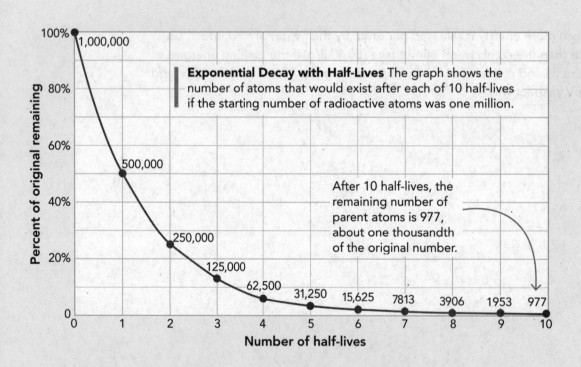

Exponential Decay with Half-Lives The graph shows the number of atoms that would exist after each of 10 half-lives if the starting number of radioactive atoms was one million.

After 10 half-lives, the remaining number of parent atoms is 977, about one thousandth of the original number.

Identify Limitations of a Model What are the limitations of the graph as a model of the radioactive decay of isotopes in nature? What are the limitations of the half-life formula?

_____

_____

_____

Mathematical Practices: Persevere in Solving Problems

Checking work is part of seeing a problem through to the end. To avoid repeating an error, it is important to check answers using a different method to solve the problem and to ask, "Does this answer make sense?"

Consider the half-life problem below. The worked-out solution is provided on the left and the process used to check the answer is given to the right.

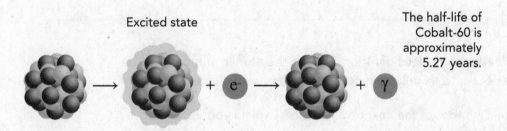

$$^{60}_{27}\text{Co} \longrightarrow {}^{60}_{28}\text{Ni*} + {}^{0}_{-1}\text{e} \longrightarrow {}^{60}_{28}\text{Ni} + \gamma\text{-photon}$$

Excited state

The half-life of Cobalt-60 is approximately 5.27 years.

Problem:

Cobalt-60 is used as a medical tracer and therapeutic agent. It decays into Nickel-60, which is not radioactive. What percentage of Cobalt-60 will remain after an 83.4 g laboratory sample of pure Cobalt-60 is stored for 18 years?

Solution:
Since half-life is given, use the half-life equation.

$$N = N_0 e^{-\frac{0.693t}{t_{\frac{1}{2}}}}$$

Define knowns and unknowns.

$t_{\frac{1}{2}} = 5.27$ years

$t = 18$ years

$N_0 = 83.4$ grams

$N = ?$

Solve and state as a percent remaining.

$$N = N_0 e^{-\frac{0.693t}{t_{\frac{1}{2}}}} = 83.4 \text{ g}\left(e^{-\frac{0.693(18\text{ yr})}{5.27\text{ yr}}}\right)$$
$$= 7.82 \text{ grams}$$

$$\% \text{ remaining} = \frac{7.82 \text{ g}}{83.4 \text{ g}} \times 100 = 9.38 \%$$

Check:
Determine the number of half-lives gone by, $n = \frac{t}{t_{1/2}}$

$$n = \frac{t}{t_{1/2}} = \frac{18 \text{ years}}{5.27 \text{ years}} = 3.42 \text{ half-lives gone by}$$

Use the number of half-lives gone by to estimate the mass remaining.
Divide the original mass by 2, repeat for a total of 4 half-lives.

83.4 grams → 41.7 grams → 20.9 grams → 10.45 grams → 5.21 grams

Since 3.42 half-lives passed, the final mass should be between 5.21 grams and 10.45 grams. The value calculated for N (7.82 g) makes sense.

3-Dimensional Review

1. SEP Developing and Using Models

The exponential decay curve of iodine-131 is shown in the graph. Iodine-131 has the half-life of 8.07 days. Describe how the graph may appear if it displayed the decay curve of sodium-24 (half-life of 15 hours). Explain your reasoning.

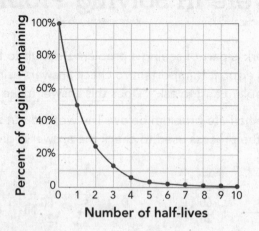

_____

_____

2. CCC Energy and Matter

A nucleus of radon-226 has the atomic number 86. The radon-226 nucleus decays to an unknown nucleus and emits an alpha particle.

a. What is the atomic number of the unknown nucleus? Explain your reasoning.

_____

_____

b. How many neutrons does the unknown nucleus have? Explain your reasoning.

_____

_____

3. DCI Nuclear Processes

Two large samples of cobalt-60 and iodine-131 go through beta decay. The half-life of cobalt-60 is 5.26 years and the half-life of iodine-131 is 8.07 days. Both samples go through one mean life. Which of the following is true?

a. Both samples are 7.59 days old.

b. The sample of cobalt-60 is 2770 days old while the sample of iodine-131 is 11.6 days old.

c. The sample of cobalt-60 is 7.59 years old while the sample of iodine-131 is 11.6 years old.

d. The sample of cobalt-60 is 3.65 years old while the sample of iodine-131 is 0.016 years old.

Skills Practice

4. Pb-206 is used to determine the age of a meteorite found on the surface of Earth. The age of the meteorite was determined to be 4.567 billion years old. Calculate the percent of the original lead-206 (^{206}Pb) that is left in the meteorite (the half-life of ^{209}Pb is 4.46×10^9 years.)

5. Archeologists discovered a sample of charcoal that was determined to be 9140 years old. Calculate the percentage of the original C-14 that is left in the charcoal. The half-life is 5730 years.

a. 55.0%

b. 33.0%

c. 78.0%

d. 22.0%

6. The mean life for isotopes of cobalt-60 is 5.26 years. What is their half-life (in years and in days)?

Radiometric Dating

A few radioisotopes can be used to date ancient materials. The isotopes must have long half-lives and they must decay into single, stable products. If there was no daughter isotope in the material when it formed, then the age equation can be used to calculate the apparent age of the material.

Age of Material
$$t = \frac{t_{1/2}}{\ln 2} \ln\left(1 + \frac{D}{P}\right)$$
t = age of material D = number of daughter isotopes
$t_{1/2}$ = half-life of material P = number of parent isotopes

The age equation assumes that all daughter isotopes formed through decay of the parent isotope. In reality, several factors can alter the number of parent and daughter isotopes in a material. Also, the original number of each isotope present is usually not known. In these situations, scientists add additional steps to the age determination process. The graph shows how scientists calibrate age estimates when using the decay of carbon-14 to nitrogen-14 to date materials.

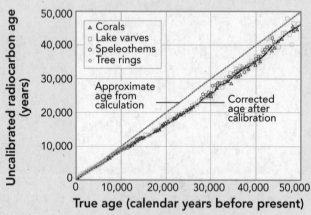

Data from: P J Reimer et al.

C-14 Calibration Curve The dashed line shows that true ages are slightly younger than uncalibrated ages. Dating methods rely on the assumption that 1 in a trillion carbon atoms in the atmosphere are C-14. But there are several factors that can cause this ratio to fluctuate, so scientists must calibrate their age measurements using carbon ratio data from other sources, such as fossilized tree rings.

Use Models Burning fossil fuels releases more C-12 into the air. This causes the ratio of C-14 to other carbon isotopes to decrease. Based on the age equation for C-14, which is $t = \left[\frac{t_{1/2}}{\ln 2}\right] \times \ln\left[\frac{P_0}{P}\right]$, will the burning of fossil fuels skew the age estimates of old objects higher or lower than their true age if the samples are contaminated with air from today's atmosphere?

_____

_____

_____

_____

Mathematical Practices: Construct Viable Arguments

Taking into consideration how data must be analyzed and qualified before it can be used as evidence is an important step in constructing viable arguments. This skill is needed when making and evaluating claims about the age and composition of ancient materials.

Radiometric dating requires comparing the number of parent isotopes (P) and daughter isotopes (D) present in a material over time. Making plausible arguments about the age of materials involves reasoning about this isotope data, recognizing that isotope types might be analyzed in different ways because the factors that influence their abundance in the environment and objects will vary. Calibration curves and the use of reference isotopes are two examples of how scientists qualify isotope data.

Scientists also qualify data as they construct arguments about space objects. For example, scientists compare the composition of Earth rocks, the sun, and ancient meteorites to make claims about the start of the solar system.

Compositions of the Meteorites and the Sun It is easy to believe that the composition of meteorites and the composition of Earth are similar because they are each made of rock. But the fact that most elements fall on the 1:1 line shows how similar the composition of the sun and meteorites are and strengthens the argument that meteorites reveal the ratio of elements present at the start of the solar system.

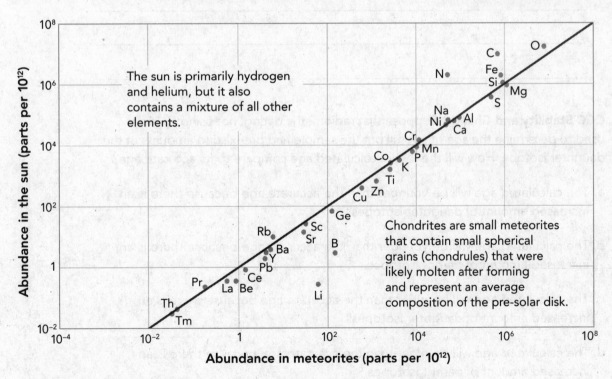

Data from: Table 1, Solar System Abundances of the Elements, H. Palme and A. Jones, volume 1, 2003, Elsevier Ltd.

3-Dimensional Review

1. **SEP Constructing Explanations and Designing Solutions** How should the composition of the moon and Earth compare to support the co-formation model for the moon? Explain your reasoning.

_____

_____

_____

2. **DCI The History of Planet Earth** Radiometric dating is used to determine the ages of meteorites. These data are also used to predict the age of Earth.

   a. Explain why the ages of meteorites can be used to determine Earth's age.

   _____

   _____

   b. Data from fossils are used to correct C-14 dating errors. How are fossils from trees and coral used to create a calibration curve to correct the C-14 data?

   _____

   _____

   _____

   _____

3. **CCC Stability and Change** Suppose that radiometric dating, not using C-14, is used to determine the age of a fossil but the sample had preexisting amounts of the daughter isotope. How will the fossil's calculated age compare to its accurate age?

   a. The calculated age will be younger than the accurate age because there is an increased amount of daughter isotopes.

   b. The calculated age will be younger than the accurate age because there is an increased amount of parent isotopes.

   c. The calculated age will be older than the accurate age because there is an increased amount of daughter isotopes.

   d. The calculated age will be older than the accurate age because there is an increased amount of parent isotopes.

Skills Practice

4. One of the oldest musical instruments yet found was a bone flute made thousands of years ago. The archaeologists performed a radiocarbon test on the bone flute. The results from the mass spectrometer show that for each gram of carbon there are about 6.22×10^{-15} g of C-14. The half-life of carbon is 5730 years. How old is the bone flute?

5. Suppose that laboratory radiometric dating gives the age of a bone as 15,000 years. Using the calibration curve, what is the actual age of the bone?

a. 12,000 years
b. 15,000 years

c. 18,000 years
d. 20,000 years

6. Two fossilized shells were compared. Using carbon dating, fossil A was calculated to be 22,000 years old. Fossil B was calculated to be 41,000 years old. Based on the calibration curve, compare the reliability of the calibration age of each fossil. Include the actual age of each fossil.

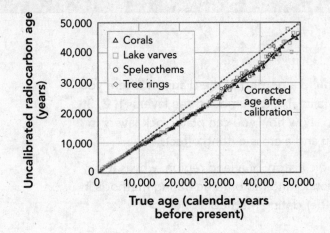

_____

_____

_____

_____

_____

Geologic Time

Understanding the geologic history of a specific location on Earth's surface involves analyzing the rock layers in that area. Using radiometric methods to date each layer would be time consuming and costly. Instead, scientists use the rules of horizontality, superposition, and crosscutting effects to establish the relative ages of different layers of exposed rock. They also use clues in the rock layers to identify catastrophic events that might have changed the land in significant ways.

Rock Layers Reveal Earth's History

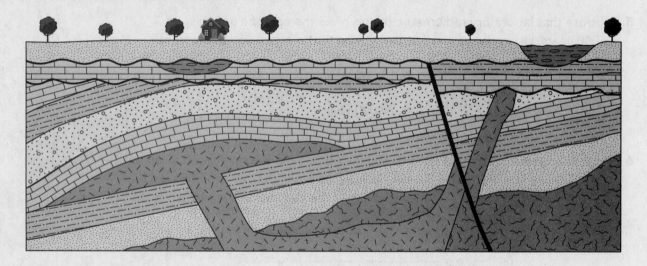

Interpret Data Place a box around a portion of the diagram where you observe an example of horizontality. Next, number three layers (1, 2, 3; youngest = 1 and oldest = 3) to show how you can place rock layers in time order due to superposition and a cross-cutting effect.

When reconstructing the geologic history of a land region, why is it more effective to use relative dating and radiometric dating methods in combination than it is to use either dating method alone?

_____

_____

_____

_____

Science Practices: Analyzing and Interpreting Data

Scientific investigations of Earth produce large data sets that must be analyzed in order to derive meaning. Because data patterns and trends are not always obvious, scientists use a variety of visualization strategies to help identify patterns in the data, such as graphs, maps, or diagrams.

Visualization is particularly useful when analyzing geologic data because the time scales involved are so large. By condensing millions and millions of years of data into a single graph or map, cycles or other patterns of change become apparent. The table describes several examples.

Visualization Strategy	Type of Data	Observed Patterns
graphs	genera on Earth (groups of species)	large declines (mass extinctions) followed by rapid diversification of species
maps	age of rocks along the ocean's lithospheric plates	youngest rocks closest to trenches
	magnetic direction of rocks alongside ocean trenches or surrounding volcanoes	alternating north-south stripes revealing pole reversals
diagrams	mineral composition of rocks	horizontal layers, slanted layers, discontinuities

Analyzing the relative positions of rock layers using diagrams allows scientists to establish a geologic history for regions on Earth. Suppose scientists were trying to determine approximate dates for when seismic activity shifted the rock layers shown in the diagram. Analysis of the diagram reveals that the fault line (K) disrupts all rock layers except layer J. Rock layer J was deposited in a horizontal layer atop the fault. By using dating methods to establish the age of the oldest (deepest) rocks in layer J, scientists can approximate a date for the earthquake that caused the fault.

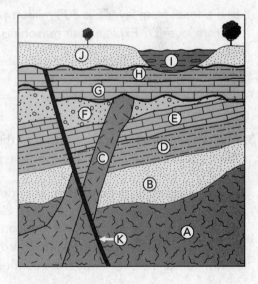

Analysis of the diagram also reveals that this geologic region had experienced previous geologic disturbances. At one time B, D, and E were horizontal layers, but their angled appearance indicates that they were displaced, perhaps by magma pushing up from underneath. This hypothesis is supported by the fact that hot magma pushed up through layers B, D, E, and F to form intrusion C.

3-Dimensional Review

1. DCI The History of Planet Earth Two groups of archeologists collect samples of Earth's crust. Group A digs deeper into Earth as group B moves from the edge of the continental crust towards the mid-ocean ridge. Compare the relative age of the samples they collect. Which group will find the oldest samples?

2. SEP Engaging in Argument from Evidence

Five different fossils were collected from the layers shown in the image.

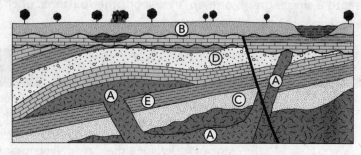

a. Using relative dating, create an argument for the relative ages of the layers shown. List the layers in order from youngest to oldest, with youngest on the far left. Explain your reasoning.

b. If a fossil from layer E is 300 million years old, what is its age relative to a fossil from layer D? Explain your reasoning.

3. CCC Patterns How is the pattern of the ages of rock within ocean crust similar to the pattern of the ages of the different rock types that make up continental crust?

a. The rocks of both oceanic and continental crust are older with depth.

b. Oceanic rock is younger with horizontal distance away from mid-ocean ridges and the different rock types that form continental crust are younger with horizontal distance away from continental rifts.

c. Oceanic rock is younger with horizontal distance toward mid-ocean ridges and some continents have different rock types that are younger with horizontal distance, moving from their centers toward their edges.

d. Neither can be accurately dated using radiometric methods.

Skills Practice

4. How does a map of the ocean lithosphere describe motion and age of the oceanic crust?

_____

_____

_____

5. In a region of highly active volcanoes, what data may be necessary to determine the relative age of the rocks around the lava bed?

a. The rock samples can be analyzed in the lab for their paleomagnetism since the solidified magma records the direction of the magnetic field.

b. The rock samples can be analyzed in the lab for both their relative age since the lava bed may contain fossils from below the surface of Earth.

c. The rock samples can be compared using their location through superposition since the lava bed is now layered above the surface of Earth.

d. The rock samples can be compared using their distance from mid-ocean ridges since the lava originated from the ridges and records properties of the magnetic field.

6. An archaeologist created a graph of data to show the number of species during the Triassic, Jurassic and Cretaceous periods. The graph showed time intervals with a large increase in species after short periods of a steep decrease in species. Following this pattern, what could the archaeologist expect to observe in the fossil record during the steep decrease of species and large increase of species? Explain your reasoning.

_____

_____

_____

_____

_____

_____

The Sun

The sun is an average-sized star that gives off a tremendous amount of electromagnetic energy because of the fusion of hydrogen in its core. The energy is generated by the conversion of mass into energy according to the equation $E = mc^2$. Fusion in the sun involves a series of steps called the proton-proton I reaction.

Step 1 Protons fuse to produce deuterium (^{2}H), positrons (e^+), and neutrinos (ν_e)

Step 2 Deuterium (^{2}H) combines with protons to produce ^{3}He and gamma radiation

Step 3 ^{3}He nuclei combine producing a helium nucleus (^{4}He) and high energy protons

Net equation: $4(^1\text{H}) \rightarrow {}^4\text{He} + 2e^+ + 2\nu_e + 26.7 \text{ MeV}$

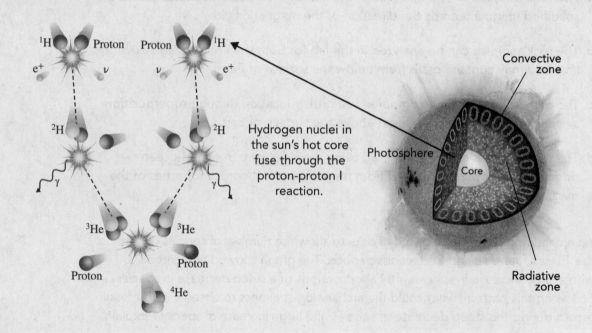

Hydrogen nuclei in the sun's hot core fuse through the proton-proton I reaction.

The gamma rays emitted during the proton-proton I reaction are absorbed and reemitted by ions in the dense plasma that makes up the sun's radiative zone. About 70% of the way to the sun's surface, the gamma rays reach the convective zone. The temperatures in this layer of the sun are cool enough for hydrogen atoms to form, which absorb the gamma rays and transfer energy to the sun's outermost layers in large convection cells. In the photosphere, hydrogen atoms ionize by gaining electrons. These ions absorb and reemit photons, generating light that travels through the sun's outermost layers. This is the light that travels through space to Earth and that provides energy for life processes.

Use Models The helium nucleus that forms in the proton-proton I reaction includes two neutrons. According to the model, what is the origin of these neutrons?

_____

_____

Mathematical Practices: Look for Repeated Reasoning

Many nuclear processes take place in a series of steps. Looking for what calculations you need to repeat can help you calculate the total energy produced or the mass destroyed during a nuclear reaction.

For example, repeated reasoning is needed to determine the total energy released during the proton-proton I reaction.

Step	Energy Released	Repeats?	Total Energy
two ^{1}H fuse to form ^{2}H (e^+ and ν_e released)	1.442 MeV	2×	2.884 MeV
^{2}H combines with a proton to form ^{3}He (γ radiation released)	5.490 MeV	2×	10.980 MeV
two ^{3}He fuse to form ^{4}He (2 protons released)	12.859 MeV	1×	12.859 MeV
		Total Energy	26.723 MeV

Repeated reasoning is also useful when determining the elements that form when stars run out of hydrogen and begin fusing helium. When stars are very, very hot, three helium nuclei (^{4}He) fuse to produce ^{12}C, and then ^{12}C can fuse again with helium to produce ^{18}O. This oxygen nucleus can also fuse with helium, producing ^{20}Ne. The addition of a helium nucleus can happen again and again (up to the formation of ^{52}Fe) forming an abundance of elements with nuclei that are integer multiples of the ^{4}He nucleus. The sun will not begin this "helium burning" process for another 5 billion years.

Analyzing cyclical patterns on graphs also requires repeated reasoning. Consider how the number of sunspots varies with the sun's apparent brightness.

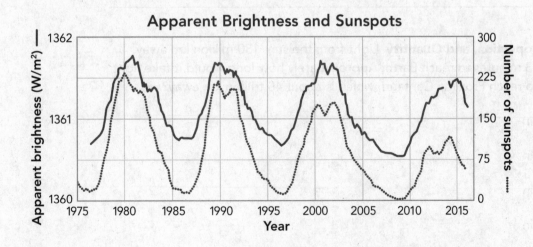

By comparing the approximate dates for each set of peaks on the graph, you can conclude that the apparent brightness and number of sunspots increase together every 10 to 15 years during the time period presented.

3-Dimensional Review

1. DCI The Universe and Its Stars If the sun provides light and energy to all of the planets in our solar system, why is there not life on those planets?

_____

_____

_____

_____

2. SEP Developing and Using Models

  a. According to the proton-proton chain model, how does the sun produce energy?

    _____

    _____

  b. In what layer of the sun is nuclear fusion occurring? What does this indicate about the temperature and pressure needed for the process?

    _____

    _____

  c. Based on this model, how many hydrogen atoms would be needed to produce 213.6 MeV?

    _____

    _____

    _____

3. CCC Scale, Proportion, and Quantity Light from the sun, 150 million km away, takes about 8.3 minutes to reach Earth. Approximately how long would it take light from the sun to reach Proxima Centauri, which is about 40 trillion km away?

  a. 4.1×10^3 min

  b. 2.1×10^3 min

  c. 2.2×10^6 min

  d. 5.1×10^9 min

Skills Practice

4. Calculate how much mass, in atomic mass units (amu), is destroyed per starting nucleon in the triple-alpha process to make one ^{12}C nucleus. Use 1 amu = 931.5 MeV/c^2 for the mass of a nucleon.

$$^4\text{He} + {}^4\text{He} \rightarrow {}^8\text{Be} - 0.0918 \text{ MeV}$$

$$^8\text{Be} + {}^4\text{He} \rightarrow {}^{12}\text{C} + 2\gamma + 7.367 \text{ MeV}$$

5. Calculate how much mass, in atomic mass units (amu), is destroyed per starting nucleon in the nuclear fusion process to make one ^{16}O nucleus and a ^{24}Mg nucleus. Use 1 amu = 931.5 MeV/c^2 for the mass of a nucleon.

$$^8\text{Be} + {}^4\text{He} \rightarrow {}^{12}\text{C} + 2\gamma + 7.367 \text{ MeV}$$

$$^{12}\text{C} + {}^{12}\text{C} \rightarrow {}^{20}\text{Ne} + {}^4\text{He} + 4.617 \text{ MeV}$$

$$2({}^{20}\text{Ne}) \rightarrow {}^{16}\text{O} + {}^{24}\text{Mg} + 4.590 \text{ MeV}$$

6. If 0.00265 amu is destroyed per starting nucleon in this nuclear fusion reaction to make one ^{4}He nucleus, choose the option that identifies the energy released in stage two. Use 1 amu = 931.5 MeV/c^2 for the mass of a nucleon.

$$^3\text{He} + {}^4\text{He} \rightarrow {}^7\text{Be} + \gamma + 1.59 \text{ MeV}$$

$$^7\text{Be} + e \rightarrow {}^7\text{Li} + \nu_e + \underline{\quad\quad}$$

$$^7\text{Li} + {}^1\text{H} \rightarrow 2({}^4\text{He}) + 17.35 \text{ MeV}$$

a. 0.403 MeV   **b.** 0.808 MeV

c. 1.61 MeV   **d.** 2.61 MeV

Stars

Fusion reactions inside stars produce elements. Stars fuse hydrogen first to form helium. When the hydrogen runs out, the star's temperature rises and helium fusion begins. The temperature must increase for ^{8}Be to combine with another ^{4}He nucleus to form ^{12}C. This is called the triple-alpha process. When stars expand into red giants, they fuse even heavier elements than carbon through the alpha ladder.

Fusion in the Core of a Supergiant

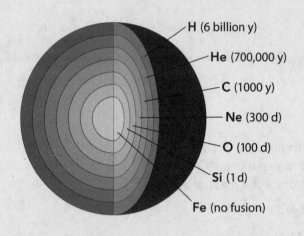

H (6 billion y)
He (700,000 y)
C (1000 y)
Ne (300 d)
O (100 d)
Si (1 d)
Fe (no fusion)

Fusion on the alpha ladder happens very quickly in layers within the core, just before the star explodes as a supernova.

The elements formed have nuclei that are integer multiples of the ^{4}He nucleus. The larger the star, the higher up the alpha ladder its fusion products can go.

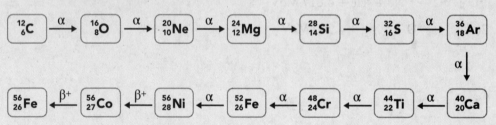

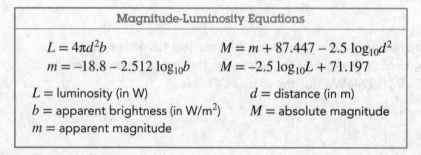

The fusion process in stars also generates light. Luminosity is the rate at which light is emitted from a star. Scientists compare star brightness on a logarithmic scale called magnitude. The more negative the magnitude, the *greater* a star's luminosity.

Magnitude-Luminosity Equations	
$L = 4\pi d^2 b$	$M = m + 87.447 - 2.5 \log_{10} d^2$
$m = -18.8 - 2.512 \log_{10} b$	$M = -2.5 \log_{10} L + 71.197$

L = luminosity (in W) d = distance (in m)
b = apparent brightness (in W/m^2) M = absolute magnitude
m = apparent magnitude

Explain Phenomena Why are the heaviest elements formed closest to the center of a star's core?

_____

_____

Mathematical Practices: Model with Mathematics

The sun has a luminosity (L) equal to 3.846×10^{26} watts. To find its absolute magnitude (M), choose the equation that relates L and M.

$$M = -2.5 \log_{10} L + 71.197$$
$$M_{sun} = -2.5 \log_{10} (3.846 \times 10^{26} \text{ W}) + 71.197 = 4.7$$

In comparison, Betelgeuse is 10 times more massive than the sun and has an absolute magnitude of –5.6. The mass and luminosity of stars can vary by several orders of magnitude. For this reason, graphs that compare these star characteristics use logarithmic scales.

A logarithmic scale is a nonlinear scale that increases incrementally by a factor of a logarithm base. The graph comparing star intensity with light wavelength uses a base 10 logarithmic scale on both the x- and y-axes. Identifying the scales used on a graph is an important first step in interpreting how the variables plotted change relative to each other.

Color as a Function of Temperature

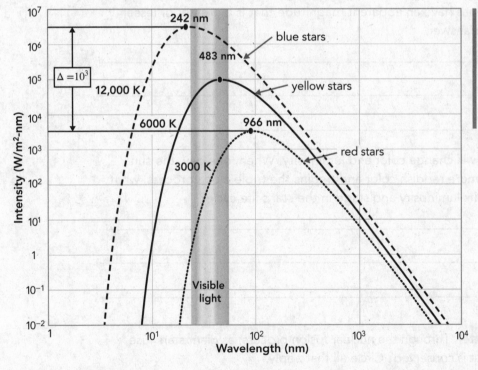

Stars radiate energy according to a blackbody spectrum. The color of a star is an indication of its temperature, which is also an indication of its total luminosity.

Notice that the gridlines on the x-axis are spaced farther apart than on the y-axis. The light wavelengths emitted by stars vary over a much smaller range given their unit of measurement compared to how intensity varies. By taking into consideration the logarithmic scale on the x-axis, it becomes clearer that the visible light energy we can see from stars is only a fraction of the electromagnetic energy that stars release.

3-Dimensional Review

1. DCI The Universe and Its Stars In your own words, describe the difference between the apparent magnitude and the absolute magnitude of a star. What is the purpose of having both?

_____

_____

_____

_____

2. SEP Obtain, Evaluate, and Communicate Information

a. According to the Magnitude-Luminosity equations, how are luminosity and apparent brightness mathematically related?

_____

b. One of the objects with the greatest apparent brightness in our solar system is Venus. Would Venus have an apparent magnitude that is a greater or lesser value? Explain your answer.

_____

_____

_____

c. As the sun ages, it will change color and luminosity. When, one day, the sun appears to have a more reddish color and begins the triple alpha process, what will that say about its luminosity and stage in the star's life cycle?

_____

_____

_____

3. CCC Energy and Matter Through the nuclear fusion process, as giant stars fuse heavier elements, what is conserved? Circle all that apply.

a. total number of atoms

b. total energy

c. total number of electrons

d. total number of protons and neutrons

Skills Practice

4. The brightest star in Earth's night sky, Sirius A, is about 8.6 ly away from Earth. The star has an apparent brightness, as seen from Earth, of 1.29×10^{-7} W/m². Calculate Sirius A's luminosity (L), apparent magnitude (m), and absolute magnitude (M).

5. Vega is a star that is about 25.05 ly away from Earth. The star has an apparent brightness, as seen from Earth, of 3.19×10^{-8} W/m². Calculate Vega's luminosity (L), apparent magnitude (m), and absolute magnitude (M).

6. Rigel is a star that is about 864.3 ly away from Earth. The star has an apparent magnitude of 0.12. Calculate Rigel's absolute magnitude (M).

a. $M = -7.0$

b. $M = -2.8$

c. $M = -0.1$

d. $M = 4.3$

The Big Bang

Three primary lines of evidence support the Big Bang theory: the cosmological redshift of distant stars and galaxies, the cosmic microwave background, and the composition of the universe. Scientists can observe the expanding universe by examining the supernovae of white dwarfs in other galaxies. A plot of a galaxy's velocity away from Earth versus its distance, d, shows a linear relationship with a slope called the Hubble constant, $H = \frac{v}{d}$.

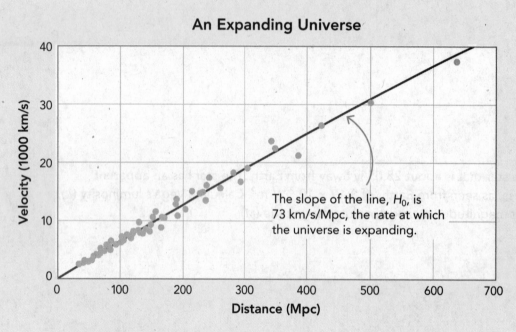

An Expanding Universe

The slope of the line, H_0, is 73 km/s/Mpc, the rate at which the universe is expanding.

Hubble's Law By examining the supernovae of white dwarfs in other galaxies, a linear relationship between a galaxy's distance and its speed away from Earth is evident.

The universe evolved most rapidly during its first minutes, so everyday physical processes have been in place and unchanging for approximately 98% of the universe's history. Yet, ordinary matter comprises only 5% of the total mass of the universe. The rest of the universe is made up of dark matter and dark energy. Dark energy is constantly increasing and working against the pull of gravity, so it is unlikely that the universe could ever condense back into a tiny dense point that contains all matter, space, and time.

Use Graphs Suppose the distance between a galaxy and Earth increases by 100 Mpc. According to the graph, how will the galaxy's velocity away from Earth change during the same time period?

Mathematical Practices: Construct Viable Arguments

The patterns that scientists observe in the density of radiation, matter, and dark energy in the universe are helpful when constructing arguments about the future of the universe. As the graph shows, the universe is now dominated by dark energy. The radiation density and matter density in the universe are decreasing while the dark energy remains constant. Notice that the x- and y-axes on the graph use different logarithmic scales. The matter density and radiation density of the universe have changed by several orders of magnitude over the long history of the universe.

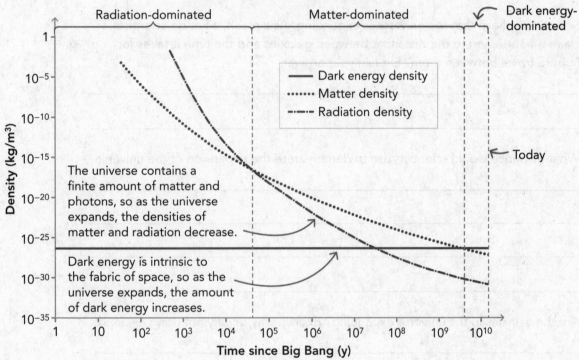

Three Stages of the Universe

Consider how the information presented in the graph refutes the idea that the universe might experience a "big crunch" due to gravity.

Claim: The universe cannot experience a "big crunch" due to gravity.

Evidence: The density of matter in the universe is decreasing, spreading apart as the universe expands. The density of dark energy is not changing as the universe expands, so the amount of dark energy in the universe is increasing. Dark energy works against the pull of gravity.

Reasoning: Since matter is spreading out, the gravitational pull between massive objects in the universe is decreasing. Also, dark energy works against gravity and is increasing. So, there are at least two factors preventing the contraction (shrinking) of the universe over time.

3-Dimensional Review

1. DCI The Universe and Its Stars Explain in your own words how the chemical composition of the universe supports the Big Bang theory.

_____

_____

_____

_____

2. SEP Constructing Explanations and Designing Solutions

a. Scientists believe that the universe is expanding. As a result, what do scientists claim is happening to the distances between galaxies and the time it takes for light to travel between them? Explain your answer.

_____

_____

b. What evidence would scientists use to demonstrate the expansion of the universe?

_____

_____

_____

_____

c. Are the galaxies in the universe expanding? Explain why or why not using evidence.

_____

_____

_____

_____

3. CCC Energy and Matter Of the phenomena listed, which of the following contradicts the conservation of energy?

a. the creation of dark energy　　　**b.** Big Bang nucleosynthesis

c. the Boson emergence　　　**d.** the cosmological redshift

Skills Practice

4. Using the radiation density equation, calculate the mass density of radiation in the universe when the temperature was about 1.0×10^9 K. What time period was this likely in? How do you know?

5. Using the radiation density equation, calculate the mass density of radiation in the universe when the temperature was about 314 K. What time period was this likely in? How do you know?

6. Which of the following temperatures of the universe coincide with the dark energy-dominated era?

   a. 2910 K   **b.** 291 K

   c. 29.1 K   **d.** 2.91 K

Notes

Notes

Notes

Notes

Notes

Notes

Notes

Notes

Notes

Notes

Notes

Notes

Notes

Notes

Notes